PENGUIN BOOKS

THE WALKING DIET

Les Snowdon is a manager in the oil industry. He has been an enthusiastic walker since childhood and in recent years has been interested in the fitness and slimming benefits that walking can bring to people of all ages. Les is also particularly interested in what he calls 'inner walking' and 'walking meditation'. He believes that fitness of the spirit is just as important as fitness of the body.

Maggie Humphreys teaches French at a prep school in Wimbledon; she is also a 'musical guide dog' for a blind harpsicordist. An enthusiastic cook, Maggie is interested in everything to do with cooking and nutrition. Like many women, she has tried several dieting plans, but the Walking Diet has proved to be the most effective and promises the best long-term benefits for health, fitness and slimming.

LES SNOWDON AND
MAGGIE HUMPHREYS

THE WALKING DIET

WALK BACK TO FITNESS IN THIRTY DAYS

PENGUIN BOOKS

PENGUIN BOOKS

Published by the Penguin Group
Penguin Books Ltd, 27 Wrights Lane, London W8 5TZ, England
Penguin Books USA Inc., 375 Hudson Street, New York, New York 10014, USA
Penguin Books Australia Ltd, Ringwood, Victoria, Australia
Penguin Books Canada Ltd, 10 Alcorn Avenue, Toronto, Ontario, Canada M4V 3B2
Penguin Books (NZ) Ltd, 182–190 Wairau Road, Auckland 10, New Zealand

Penguin Books Ltd, Registered Offices: Harmondsworth, Middlesex, England

First published by Mainstream Publishing Company (Edinburgh) Ltd 1991
Published in Penguin Books 1992
1 3 5 7 9 10 8 6 4 2

Illustrations by Mark Steadman.

The publishers would like to thank the following for permission to reproduce copyright
material: Table 2, p. 19, copyright © Newsweek, 13 November 1989, *Journal of the
American Medical Association*; 'The Moor', p. 186, copyright © R. S. Thomas.
In addition, the fat and fibre contents for foods are taken from the official UK food tables
which are published as *The Composition of Foods*, fourth edition, and its supplements. The
tables are being revised and expanded in a collaboration between the Ministry of
Agriculture, Fisheries and Food and the Royal Society of Chemistry. The following
supplements expand and revise the data in the fourth edition (1978): *Immigrant Foods*,
(HMSO, 1985); *Cereals and Cereal Products* (RSC/MAFF, 1988); *Milk Products and Eggs*
(RSC/MAFF, 1989).

The moral right of the authors has been asserted

Printed in England by Clays Ltd, St Ives plc

To
J. A. S. and E. A. H.
with love

CONTENTS

Walking is the best medicine
HIPPOCRATES

I have two doctors, my left leg and my right
G. M. TREVELYAN

Not running, not jogging, but walking is your most efficient exercise and the only one you can safely follow all the years of your life
QUARTERLY REPORT
— EXECUTIVE HEALTH ORGANISATION, CALIFORNIA

The land of our better selves is most surely reached by walking
H. I. BROCK

The longest journey starts with just one step
TAO TE CHING

CHAPTER 1

INTRODUCTION

Of all exercises walking is the best
THOMAS JEFFERSON

In one sense you could say that we begin our lives in the wheelchair of the womb; we begin our lives literally by being carried around. In fact it would be true to say that many of us spend most of our lives being carried around.

As we leave the womb, enter the world and grow, and get over the initial wonder of walking, we change our pre-natal wheelchair for a series of substitute wheelchairs – bicycles, motor-cycles, cars, taxis, buses, trains, aeroplanes – and chairs (in houses, schools, offices; anywhere where people gather and sit).

For this is the age of 'homo sedentarius' (sedentary man), the man who sits. In all ages prior to our modern scientific age, people had a more physical and active lifestyle. They spent more time on their feet than they did sitting.

But this is no longer true. The table below, derived from a 1985 study of Welsh adults, shows the extent to which all of us become increasingly sedentary as we get older. The figures can be taken as generally representative for both Europe and the USA.

By their mid-40s, more than 40 per cent of males and more than 80 per cent of females are sedentary. And through all age groups for women

(12–64), two-thirds of them take very little exercise at all.

TABLE 1

Age	Percentage sedentary or minimally active at work or play	
	Males	Females
12–17	13.5	27.0
18–24	17.0	54.5
25–34	25.0	67.0
35–44	32.5	72.5
45–54	41.5	81.0
55–64	57.0	86.0
Total 12–64	32.0	66.5

But there is evidence that this pattern is changing.

As the 1980s came to an end the fitness movement worldwide had become a £1 billion industry. The National Sports Goods Survey and other surveys estimate that 25 million people exercise regularly in Britain and the USA. And the General Household Survey in Britain informs us that 3 million women now participate regularly in keepfit, yoga and aerobics.

The 80s had been all about obsessional lifestyles, body consciousness, diet fads, work-out videos, designer leotards, Reeboks and Aqua Libra. As the 80s came to an end, punishing exercise routines had become almost an alternative religion for many people. For the first time exercise was an end in itself.

However, despite these encouraging figures, marketing studies carried out in the USA show that most home-gym equipment goes unused and only around 10 per cent of American adults engage in brisk, regular exercise. And in Britain, the last survey carried out by the Sports Council revealed that up to 75 per cent of the population were doing very little at all to get fit. Other surveys show that Britain as a nation is no fitter than it was ten years ago.

So the increased interest in fitness may not be the healthy trend that it first appeared to be.

EXERCISE – THE FINAL FRONTIER

For more than two decades now, first one, then another exercise programme has been thrust at us as the answer to all the ills of modern living from heart attacks to stress. We have been preached to by film stars and eastern gurus; by so called fitness experts and by celebrities who want to tell us how to maintain youthful looks. Books on jogging, cycling, swimming, rowing, aerobics, and various exercise routines all crowd the bookshelves clamouring for our attention. Yet how many people who buy all these books are still actively following the exercise programmes laid out in them?

And what have all these books been telling us to do?

TO JOG – Jogging is popular and many claim it is the best way to exercise. We have all seen the new jogger in his designer track suit and shoes, puffing and panting along the pavement, joints creaking and heart pounding as though his life depended upon it. But the truth is that it is easy to overdo jogging. Jogging has a high failure rate with beginners, and is the cause of numerous painful injuries. Ankle strain, foot strain, stress fractures, strained knee ligaments and inflammation of the Achilles tendon are all common injuries suffered by joggers. And don't forget, the arch-guru of jogging himself, Jim Fixx, dropped dead in the end – while jogging!

TO SWIM – Swimming is claimed to be an excellent way to exercise, but unless you have regular access to a swimming pool, it's unlikely that you will ever be able to swim enough to gain any real benefit from it. And water does not allow the full natural movement of the body under the force of gravity which is needed to develop and retain structural strength in the bones.

TO CYCLE – Cycling avoids the excess strain that running puts on the joints, but tends to over-develop the leg muscles. Getting out in the open air on a bike can be an exhilarating experience. It is aerobic and helps build stamina but it is difficult and potentially dangerous in traffic; and like jogging it is easy to overdo. Stationary exercise bikes are no better, with the need for long periods of hamster-like moronic trundling to get any real benefits from them. Some people reckon to do half an hour every day. Good luck to them. Ten minutes, in our experience, is enough to bore anyone out of their mind.

Other enthusiasts have been trying to persuade us to do aerobics, skip, row and a dozen other things to keep fit. Exercise and fitness has become the final frontier.

Whatever next?

Maggie and I were no different to anyone else. The 1980s had left us both with spreading waistlines and a feeling that we were beginning to slow down. Like many people around 40 we desperately needed a programme for diet and exercise that would fit in with our busy lifestyles.

Yet we knew that if a programme was going to work it had to be 'user friendly' – we had had enough of diet and exercise books written by doctors and self-proclaimed experts. We did not have the time to visit the swimming-pool three times a week, and we were not interested in pumping iron or trundling around on an exercise bike every morning.

We had tried to combine exercise with a healthy diet. We both played tennis and squash and most weekends we would walk in the countryside, on the hills or along the seashore. We had tried cycling, skipping and jogging and we both had an exercise bike in the spare room. But like many people we had sustained injuries and we had finally become disillusioned about ever becoming fit.

We felt that our diet was reasonably balanced. We had increased our fibre intake and we were eating more fish, fruit and vegetables. We had reduced our consumption of saturated fats, sugar, salt and alcohol. Neither of us smoked. And yet despite all this the pounds were creeping up on us and we seemed to be fighting a losing battle.

So what were we doing wrong?

Quite simply, like millions of other people, we had become sedentary. We were spending too much time sitting.

'But hold on,' we can hear you say, 'I thought you said that you walked on weekends and played tennis and squash.'

True. But that still makes us sedentary, like most other people. For if you are not exercising aerobically using some form of whole body continuous movement (brisk walking, jogging, cycling) for 30 minutes at least three to four times a week, then by definition, you are sedentary.

Let's say you get up in the morning and spend 15 minutes sitting down for breakfast. Then you spend another 30 minutes sitting in a car, bus or train on the way to work. When you arrive at work you may then spend another six hours sitting in a chair working. Then 30 minutes back home again and about another four hours sitting around the house before retiring to bed.

Is this an exaggeration?

Not for many people it isn't. And if you think about it, that's more than 11 hours each and every weekday. And unless you make a special effort to do something active on a weekend, then you can add another 16 hours or so to the total, making a grand total of more than 70 hours each week.

If you exclude the eight hours on average spent in bed each night, then you could be spending around 65 per cent of your entire waking life in one form of sedentary position or another. You could be described as being no more than a brain on wheels or a brain stuck in a chair.

And don't say that you are much more active than the people described above, for the sedentary label applies to most people in Western society, including club golfers, club squash and tennis players, mailmen, and Mrs Smith next door who is out in all weathers exercising her dog. The figures for percentage sedentary people at the beginning of this chapter tell only part of the story.

Being active is not enough!

If you are not regularly stretching your body aerobically in some form of continuous whole body exercise, then you are sedentary.

Join the ranks of homo sedentarius – you have a problem.

WALKING – THE BEST EXERCISE

These men I have examined around the world who live in vigorous health to 100 or more years are great walkers. If you want to live a long, long time in sturdy health you can't go wrong in forming the habit of long vigorous walking every day . . . until it becomes a habit as important to you as eating and sleeping.

Dr Leaf,
Executive Health Organisation, California

Experience tells us that many people who take up jogging, cycling, and other aerobic routines often sustain injuries, or simply give up after a short time. They join the increasing number of people who regularly try to get fit and fail.

So what are they doing wrong?

There are only two facts you need to know about exercise:

1. IF YOU DON'T DESIGN AN EXERCISE PROGRAMME FOR YOURSELF THAT REMAINS ENJOYABLE AS YOUR FITNESS IMPROVES YOU'LL QUIT!

That is why it is often only enthusiasts who are still cycling, swimming, jogging and doing aerobics. The rest of us quit a long time ago.

2. EXERCISE REALLY MEANS CONTINUING TO EXERCISE: TODAY, TOMORROW AND FOR THE REST OF YOUR LIFE.

Exercise is not a short-term cure like taking an aspirin to cure a headache. If exercise is to be effective it must become as natural to us as breathing, eating, or cleaning our teeth. Otherwise most of our efforts are all a waste of time and energy.

This is why walking scores every time:

- Walking is the best exercise – it is a totally natural activity; your enjoyment will improve as your fitness improves.
- Walking is habit-forming; the more you do it the more you will want to do it.
- Walking aerobically will give you all the fitness benefits of jogging, cycling and dance aerobics – without the injuries.
- Walking aerobically makes you slim and is the perfect weight-management system.
- Walking is simple and safe; just about anyone can do it, including the young, elderly and those recovering from illness.
- Walking is a prevention against heart and circulatory disorders and may lower blood pressure.
- Walking will help you to sleep and is an antidote to stress, nervous tension and depression.
- Walking can improve your posture and may prevent lower back pain.
- Walking requires no special skills or equipment.
- Walking can be done almost anywhere.

Regular, vigorous aerobic exercise like brisk walking can lead to beneficial physiological changes in many of the body's processes: lower blood pressure, lower cholesterol level, and improved cardiovascular and respiratory response.

Many of the benefits that come from brisk walking are due to the CV effect – the effect produced on the cardiovascular (CV) system. By gently stretching the capacity of the heart and lungs through exercise, the CV system's capacity is increased. This is what makes this type of exercise (like jogging and cycling) aerobic.

But if exercise is not kept up, the body reverts to its original inactive state. Former athletes who took no further exercise were found to have the same risk factor for a heart attack as those who had never been active. It can take three to six months of regular vigorous aerobic exercise to build up a powerful heart and lungs; and it can take the same period of inactivity to lose it all.

I began serious walking after the long hot summer of 1989. For the first time in my life I had a weight problem. I had put on around a stone during the year and I was beginning to take on the traditional pear shape. My waist size had suddenly increased and I could not get into my trousers any more.

I was determined to lose the weight. I had always loved walking so it seemed the obvious thing to do. I would simply get out more often and walk faster and for longer.

I decided on a 30-day plan. I felt that if I could get into a regular habit-forming routine then I would be able to keep it up beyond the 30 days. My plan was to increase my pace from normal (around 3 miles per hour) to brisk (3.5–4.0 miles per hour) and to walk longer and further as the weeks went by. And the key to maintaining the regularity and discipline would be to walk out of my front door and do a circuit around the block and back home again. I knew that if I had to drive to the park or into the country first, then the walking would never get done except at weekends. This was the key to the whole thing – REGULAR, RHYTHMIC BRISK WALKING OUT OF MY FRONT DOOR, AROUND THE BLOCK AND BACK AGAIN.

After two weeks I felt better in myself and I had lost several pounds. Although previously I had been walking only on weekends, I was now walking up to five times a week for half an hour at a time. I was not only losing weight but I felt better: fitter, more alert, more vigorous.

The plan was working.

After 30 days of aerobic walking and cutting down on fattening foods I had walked away half a stone. I was able to get back into some of my trousers and I was well on the way to my ultimate goal of health and fitness.

Maggie had also started to use the plan and walk her way to health and fitness. We both knew that walking alone would not keep the pounds off forever. We had to get our diet right also.

Maggie has always loved cooking and everything to do with food, so she began to put together all her low fat lean cuisine recipes and a complete diet/exercise programme evolved which would not only get rid of the pounds but keep them off forever.

And so the Walking Diet evolved.

The one thing that we decided from the outset was that calorie counting was out. No one can seriously go on counting calories all their lives. What we needed was a moderate approach that we could work with and modify to our own needs.

The ancient Greek concept of diet had impressed us both. To them 'diata' meant a way of living, a way of finding wholeness through health, fitness and correct nutrition.

This had to be the way to go. With regular brisk walking, and eating the right kinds of food, we should be fit and healthy without having to resort to extreme, fanatical exercise routines or slimming diets.

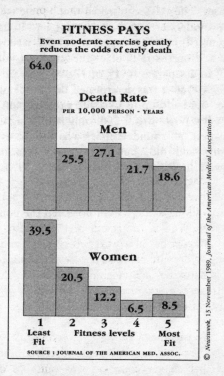

FITNESS PAYS
Even moderate exercise greatly
reduces the odds of early death

Death Rate
PER 10,000 PERSON - YEARS

Men

64.0 25.5 27.1 21.7 18.6

Women

39.5 20.5 12.2 6.5 8.5

| 1 Least Fit | 2 | 3 Fitness levels | 4 | 5 Most Fit |

SOURCE : JOURNAL OF THE AMERICAN MED. ASSOC.

Our own experiences with walking were very quickly confirmed when we read in *Time* magazine, November 1989, that after the most detailed fitness study ever carried out by the Aerobics Institute in America, it had been established that moderate exercise can have all the beneficial effects that are normally associated with hard 'no pain, no gain' exercising (see Table 2).

The *Time* report confirmed that moderate brisk walking for half an hour three to four times a week is all that is needed to provide protection not only from cardiovascular disease and cancers, but also against death from a wide range of other causes. They also confirmed that people who exercise moderately tend to live longer. It has been estimated that for every hour of brisk walking, you can add one extra hour to the length of your life.

In a separate study of 17,000 Harvard graduates in 1986 it was determined that moderate exercise could add up to two years to a person's life.

It is now official. Not only is walking the best, cheapest, all-round exercise available to everyone young and old, but it is 'green', natural and organic. It is the diet exercise for the 1990s.

CHAPTER 2

DIATA – A BETTER WAY OF LIFE

The first wealth is health
RALPH WALDO EMERSON

- In Britain there are 200,000 deaths each year from coronary heart disease – that is, nearly one every three minutes.
- In Britain there are between 500,000 and 800,000 heart attacks each year.
- In Britain one in ten men under the age of retirement will suffer a heart attack. By the age of retirement that figure will increase to one in every five.
- Britain is the world leader in deaths caused by heart disease.

Even with the improved health record of the USA and a population four to five times bigger than Britain's, more than 1 million Americans suffer a heart attack each year and more than half of them die before reaching hospital.

By anyone's standards these statistics are horrifying and are at epidemic proportions, yet there is no reason why we should accept heart disease as being inevitable.

And why is heart disease so common? Why is

there an epidemic? And why pick on heart disease alone? The UK not only has some of the highest rates of cardiovascular disease in the world, it also has some of the highest rates for cancer and respiratory disease.

And we are just as prone to other 'Western diseases' such as large bowel cancer which together with lung cancer (caused largely by smoking) are the commonest causes of death from cancer. Disease of the colon, diabetes, haemorrhoids, varicose veins, mental illness, arthritis and tooth decay all play their part in reducing the quality of life for large numbers of people each year.

And these problems are not restricted only to life in Britain, the USA and the rest of the Western world. No matter where one looks throughout the world, wherever a Western lifestyle coincides with a Western-style diet, the above effects can be observed.

CHANGING TIMES

The better off we are, the more energy rich foods we eat: meat, cheese and chocolate. And we eat more convenience foods, high in calories: burgers, pizzas, Indian and Chinese food, cakes, biscuits and pastries. A thousand million fast foods are being consumed in Britain alone every year.

In contrast to modern man, prehistoric man, 'homo erectus', was a hunter-gatherer, walking through necessity, and running to pursue and capture his prey. He had a high fibre diet and plenty of exercise. Modern man, however, homo sedentarius, does not need to pursue his food. Every type of food is readily available and preparation and cooking have never been easier; and if he cannot spare the time, convenience foods reduce the time required for shopping and preparation to the bare minimum.

But we do not have to go back to prehistoric times to witness the change in our diet. Most of the changes have taken place in the past 200 and many in the past 50 years.

We keep animals in pens to fatten them. Homo sedentarius, in contrast, does not need to be kept in pens. He accepts voluntary inactivity and as a result gets fat.

It has been observed that some people switching from using a typewriter to a personal computer can gain up to half a stone a year because they no longer have to get up to consult filing cabinets; and the same effects can be observed when people use remote-control television, extension phones, lifts and dishwashers.

And consumption of food tends to be higher in sedentary people; as a result they tend to have lower metabolic rates than active people and an increased chance of becoming even fatter. And being sedentary can increase the risk of heart disease.

Since the end of the Second World War people have been getting fatter. In Britain alone 16 million people are overweight. The population as a whole is about 10 per cent fatter than it used to be. We seem to be forever 'fighting the flab', going on crash diets, and trying to cut calories.

Yet essentially, we are what we eat. During the 20th century the average person in Western society has been eating too much fat and too little fibre. A hundred years ago the average person ate less than 25 per cent fat in their diet; today half our energy is derived from fat in different forms.

'YOU CAN'T GET FAT EXCEPT BY EATING FAT!' (Martin Katahn – *T-Factor Diet*)

In Britain, each of us gets on average 40 per cent of our calories from fat. That is bad news for our figures, and bad news for our health.

The United States Surgeon General, Dr C. Everett Koop, commented recently that FAT IS WESTERN SOCIETY'S GREATEST NUTRITIONAL HAZARD. Is it any wonder then that the Western way of eating is also the Western way of dying.

There are no simple answers as to why people suffer from cardiovascular, respiratory and other Western diseases. But various characteristics of population and lifestyle are usually blamed for the problem:

- Poor diet
- Lack of exercise
- Family history
- Obesity
- Stress
- High blood pressure
- High cholesterol level
- Alcoholism
- Smoking

All of the available evidence on lifestyle and nutrition suggests that by eating a healthier diet, exercising regularly, and finding time for relaxation, many of the above problems can be reduced if not eradicated. And a moderate approach to alcohol and the cutting out of smoking would save needless deaths and improve the quality of people's lives.

DIET AND DISEASE

Diet and disease are inseparable. If not always a causal factor, diet is always involved (Leon Chaitow – *The Stone Age Diet*). You would think from the figures for deaths and illness from Western diseases that little was being done to improve the situation.

You would be wrong.

Health education and nutritional information are widely available to everyone. Newspapers and magazines carry extensive coverage of diet and health topics and diet books are among the best sellers. In 1990 more than 25 new diet books were launched and the market is increasing. If you add to this the growing number of health and fitness related books then you would expect us all to be getting healthier and fitter.

And we are trying to become healthier. A survey released in November 1990 suggested that 90 per cent of us are trying to eat more healthily. This follows on from the 1970s and the health conscious 80s when increasing numbers of people were becoming more responsible towards themselves and their lifestyle.

Yet despite all the good intentions, health and fitness for large numbers of people are still elusive goals which seem to recede further and further away. Advertising surveys tell us that one-third of the British population uses slimming products. Other surveys tell us that 50 per cent of British women are on a diet at the moment and 25 per cent have tried three or more diets in the past year alone (*New Woman* magazine – November 1990).

People are genuinely trying to become more health conscious and fit. A 1989 Gallup Fitness Consumer Survey found that women are not only

using diets and exercise to improve their looks but
also their health.

For many people the problem of how to
become fitter and healthier is more a question of
method than intention. And that is where 'diata'
can help.

DIATA

Eating is about making choices; healthy eating is
about making the right choices. And like exercise,
it's all about balance and moderation. It's no use
taking up extreme reducing diets this week if we
end up giving them up next week. We need something we can work with today, tomorrow and the
rest of our lives.

Healthy eating is about much more than the
kinds of food we eat. It's also about lifestyle, which
affects eating habits. We like to think of it in terms
of the ancient Greek idea of 'diata' which means
literally 'a way of living'. It is both how we exercise
and what we eat that defines our 'diata'.

Diata suggests a holistic way of looking at our
health and lifestyle to find the balance and rhythm
that is lacking. When you think about it the ancient
Greeks had some pretty good ideas. The motto
engraved on the wall of the temple at Delphi was
'Know Thyself', and was adopted by the philosopher Socrates as the basis for the study of philosophy. It is also the basis for 'diata'. Know yourself: know your own body and mind; know what
your real needs are.

To listen to many authorities on nutrition, you
might think that eating is an exact science. Having
analysed the calorific value of every type of food
under the sun, they then try to organise your entire

life around their rigid schedules telling you exactly what to eat and what to avoid.

The truth is that eating is not an exact science and never will be. How many people consciously buy food each week in an organised, scientific way? Eating is not a science; it is an art. It is much more a question of knowledge and awareness of which foods to eat and which to avoid than it is of following blindly someone else's strict regime.

Knowledge, awareness, and the desire to change are the best motivations you can have. This is what diata is: a balanced, moderate approach which will provide the long-term benefits that you desire.

The biggest single change you can make in your lifestyle is to do a personal food and drink audit – an awareness audit of what you eat and drink. Write down a list of everything that you regularly eat and drink, and compare it with the following recommended lists of foods and drinks to increase and decrease. This will enable you to work out the changes you need to make in your diet and plan your own personal 'diata'.

PERSONAL FOOD AUDIT

Increase your consumption of:

OILY FISH

mackerel, herrings, pilchards, sardines, tuna, trout, salmon

WHITE FISH

cod, haddock, coley, hake, plaice, sole, turbot, monkfish

VEGETABLES

potatoes, carrots, peas, cabbage, cauliflower, broccoli,

spinach, french beans, parsnips, onions, leeks,
aubergines, courgettes, garlic, sweetcorn, asparagus

SALAD VEGETABLES
beansprouts, celery, cucumber, peppers (green/red),
radish, spring onions, chicory, lettuce, fennel,
watercress

STAPLE FOODS
beans (haricot, kidney, soya), chick peas, lentils, bread
(wholegrain), rice (wholegrain), pasta (wholemeal),
cereals (wholegrain), bran, seeds, nuts, oatbran

FRUIT
apples, pears, oranges, bananas, grapefruit, lemons,
limes, tomatoes, pineapple, avocado, guava, passion
and other exotic fruits, mango, nectarines, apricots,
dried fruit, berries

Decrease your consumption of:

SATURATED FATS

meat and meat products: beef, pork, lamb, sausages,
mince, bacon, liver, burgers, roast chicken, luncheon
meat, liver sausage (replace with lean cuts of red meat;
chicken, turkey, game); dairy products: whole milk,
cream, butter, cheese (replace with: skimmed milk, low
fat yogurt, low fat cheeses)

VEGETABLE OILS/FATS
palm oil, coconut oil, lard, dripping, suet, hard
margarine (replace with small amounts of sunflower,
safflower, corn & soya oils, olive oil, polyunsaturated
spreads)

SNACKS
crisps, peanuts, samosas

REFINED CARBOHYDRATES

sugar, chocolate, sweets, desserts,
biscuits, pastries, puddings, pies,
white bread, rolls, crackers

SALT

PERSONAL DRINK AUDIT

Increase your consumption of:

WATER

6 glasses daily

(Water is our most important nutrient; up to three-quarters of the body's weight is water. It regulates body temperature; assists all bodily functions.)

ANY LOW-CAL SOFT DRINK

Decrease your consumption of:

ALCOHOL

maximum: 3 units per day for men
2 units per day for women
(1 glass of wine, half pint beer, small whisky, each equal one unit)

Alternate with low-alcohol/alcohol-free drinks with food; drink with an equal measure of water;
try two or three AFDs – alcohol-free days – each week;
cut out altogether, if desired.

COFFEE

Drink weaker, without milk, or with skimmed milk;
try decaffeinated.

TEA

Try weak Darjeeling or any other tea, or herb or
lemon tea, or try decaffeinated.

A NEW BALANCE

A good diet should maintain health, provide
energy, promote growth, and give protection
against disease.

According to a report by the UK National
Advisory Committee on Nutritional Education
(NACNE) our total energy consumption should
be derived from the following food sources:

Carbohydrate	55%
Fat	30%
Protein	11%
Alcohol	4%

The United States Select Committee on Nutrition
and Human Needs makes similar recommenda-
tions:

Carbohydrate	55-60%
Fat	25-30%
Protein	15%

The important thing to remember is that we should
all be seeking to eat more of the right kinds of
food (foods with health and nutritional properties)
rather than seeking to fit in with someone else's
ideal consumer. Using the personal food and drink
audit we should be seeking a new balance in our
diet that will provide us with all the essential nutrients that our bodies need.

We need nutrients for energy, cell growth,
organ function, and efficient food utilisation. The
six important nutrients are carbohydrates, proteins,
fats, vitamins, minerals and water. Macronutrients

(carbohydrates, protein and fat) need micronutrients (vitamins and minerals) to release the energy contained in them. During digestion, enzymes then break these nutrients down so that they can be absorbed through the walls of the digestive tract and enter the bloodstream.

Using the personal food and drink audit, Walking Dieters will be provided with all the essential nutrients that they need. Water has already been covered in the audit; fats, proteins and carbohydrates are covered below in the section 'Where to Begin'. Now just a few words about vitamins and minerals.

Vitamins are natural substances vital for growth and health. They cannot be manufactured by our bodies. Some are needed for the efficient action of enzymes; others form essential parts of hormones. The most important thing to know about them is that they work synergistically with minerals: that is they enhance each other, adding up to more than the individual sum of their parts. We need them all.

The most important vitamins are the water soluble and fat soluble vitamins. Water soluble vitamins are the range of B vitamins (B1, B2, B3, B5, B6, B12) and vitamin C. The B vitamins are found in the staple foods (wholemeal bread, brown rice, pulses, oat bran, nuts, grains) and meat, fish, eggs, milk, poultry, green vegetables, bananas and cheese. Vitamin C is found in green, leafy vegetables, potatoes, tomatoes, fruits and berries.

The B vitamins are often called the 'stress vitamins'. They are essential for a healthy nervous system and they give protection against infection, aid in energy production and promote growth. Vitamin C is also required by those under stress and smokers, and it is important for the growth and repair of cells, gums, blood vessels, bones and teeth. And it helps in healing disease.

Both B and C vitamins, being water soluble, cannot be stored in the body and must be replaced daily. However, the fat soluble vitamins – A, D, E & K – can be stored in the body and these can be found in root vegetables, spinach, cheese, milk, eggs, fish, fish oils, dairy foods, nuts, green vegetables, and cereals. They promote growth, give protection from infections, and are essential for other body functions. The important minerals are calcium, zinc, iron, potassium, magnesium, phosphorous and iodine. Other minerals required by the body are selenium, manganese, sodium, and other trace elements. Like vitamins, they cannot be manufactured by the body, so they must be provided in our daily diet. They can be found in milk, cheese, soya beans, seafood, poultry, green vegetables, meat, eggs, nuts, beans, seeds, oat bran, citrus fruits, apples, bananas, and potatoes.

If you follow the Walking Diet you will get the vitamins and minerals that you need. However, anyone who is on the move, under stress or is likely to skip meals should think about taking a multi-vitamin and mineral supplement to make up for any deficiencies in diet. Remember that the B vitamins and vitamin C cannot be stored in your body. They need replacing every day.

WHERE TO BEGIN

• START BY REDUCING FAT

Each fat gram that you eat contains 9 calories. Each protein and carbohydrate gram you eat contains 4 calories. It is the fat in your diet that makes you fat. Our bodies are designed to burn carbohydrates and store fats.

The important thing is not to count calories, but to recognise those foods which are fat-dense. It is fat-awareness not calorie-awareness that is needed.

The main thing to cut is saturated fat which can cause high blood cholesterol levels, leading to clogged up arteries and potentially a heart attack or stroke. Saturated fat is found in fats of animal origin such as red meat, butter, milk, cheese and cream. Use skimmed or semi-skimmed milk, margarine low in saturated fats, low fat cheese, reduced calorie mayonnaise and low fat yogurt instead of cream. And try to avoid frying food wherever possible, cutting out fat, and using an oil for cooking which is low in saturated fat and high in polyunsaturates – sunflower, corn and soya oil.

The body actually needs fat. In order to grow and function effectively, fat is needed by the brain, muscles, heart, hair, skin, immune system, and cell walls, etc. The problem is that we have got the balance wrong. What we need is an oil change!

Research done among the Greenland Eskimos has shown that they have almost no record of heart disease. This is because the key factor in their diet is the amount of seafood they eat daily. Seafood contains Omega-3 fatty acids. These particular fatty acids can play a significant role in preventing heart disease and clogged up arteries. High levels of these fish oils can be found in mackerel, herrings, pilchards, sardines, tuna, trout and salmon.

Research recently carried out by the Medical Research Council in Cardiff involved 2,033 men under 70 who had suffered a heart attack. One group of men was told to eat foods rich in Omega-3 fatty acids at least twice a week. After two years it was found that the fish eaters had up to 30 per cent less chance of dying from a second heart attack than those who had been told nothing about fish.

Fat from a land based diet is known as Omega-6. The best advice now available is to cut down on Omega-6 fats and balance them with Omega-3 fish oils.

A word about cholesterol. Cholesterol has had a bad press. Although it can be responsible for a variety of illnesses, it is actually essential for health.

We now know that there are two types of cholesterol – LDL and HDL (low density and high density lipoproteins). Lipoproteins are agents in the blood which transport cholesterol. The higher your HDL level the less chance you have of developing heart disease. It is interesting to note that Eskimos have higher HDLs. This is due to their large consumption of Omega-3 fatty acids which contain the polyunsaturated fats EPA (eicosapentaenoic acid) and DHA (docosahexoenic acid). The other beneficial effects of these fish oils have already been observed above.

It has also been observed that moderate alcohol drinkers (two glasses of wine, beer or whisky a day) have higher levels of HDLs in their blood; so it seems that a small tipple each day may actually be good for you. And moderate exercise (such as brisk walking) has also been shown to raise HDLs.

Cholesterol is raised by saturated fats, sugar, coffee, food additives, the pill, stress, and lack of exercise.

• REDUCE REFINED CARBOHYDRATES

Carbohydrates, along with fats and proteins, are the three main building blocks of life. Carbohydrates are compounds of carbon, hydrogen and oxygen and their function is to provide energy. There are two types: simple and complex, or sugar and starches.

Simple carbohydrates are digested quickly, while complex ones are digested slowly, which means they can provide more energy and stamina. Some carbohydrates in a Western diet, such as sugar and syrup, are refined and provide little food value.

Sugar has been described as 'pure, white and deadly'. In Britain we eat, on average, over 100 lb (50 kg) a year each. It provides energy but hardly any nutrients. If we cut it out of our diet today we will be none the worse off but will have a head start in reducing our total intake of calories: 100 LB OF SUGAR CONVERTS ROUGHLY INTO 3,500 CALORIES A WEEK. (3,500 calories is equal to 1lb of fat – 1lb every week that you would not have to lose if you gave up sugar.)

But remember, sugar does not only come out of a packet. Two thirds of our annual consumption is hidden in processed foods such as cakes, biscuits, custard, tinned fruit, beer and fizzy drinks. Even some brands of muesli contain up to 25 per cent sugar. Almost all tinned foods contain sugar. So watch the labels. And don't forget chocolate. Britain has the highest chocolate consumption in the world, far more than any other country. The British munch through 533,000 tons – £3.5 billion worth – each year. The average consumer now eats six chocolate bars a week.

Eating refined carbohydrates such as those above can raise the blood cholesterol level, and is a possible cause of heart disease.

Other refined carbohydrates, such as white flour and white rice, like sugar, have been stripped of most of their vitamins, minerals and fibre con-

tent and should be replaced with unrefined staple
foods such as listed in the Personal Food Audit.

• REDUCE PROTEIN

Proteins are divided into two types: animal and
vegetable. Animal protein, or first class protein as
it is known, contains all eight essential amino acids
which the body depends on for good health. Vegetable protein, or second class protein, lacks some
of these amino acids, the one exception being soya
beans.

In our Western diet we eat more than twice
as much protein as we need, and of an unhealthy
type. We should cut down on red meat, always
choose lean cuts and eat more white meats, such
as chicken and turkey. We should also eat more
fish. Fish is an excellent, low calorie source of
protein. 100g (4 oz) of cooked white fish provides
one third of our total daily requirements for less
than 100 calories. Fish is also a rich source of
vitamins and minerals which the body needs and
we have already seen above the benefits obtained
by eating fish containing Omega-3 fatty acids.

As long as all the amino acids are present, all
protein is ultimately the same. If pulses (the bean
family) are combined with nuts and grains, or seeds
(sunflower, pumpkin, sesame, etc.) then the body
should be under no risk of protein deficiency. But
people who wish to reduce animal protein by
including some vegetarian dishes in their diet
should make sure that they include eggs. Eggs are
the perfect protein, containing all eight essential
amino acids, so they can make up for any
deficiency that may be caused elsewhere.

• INCREASE FIBRE

Fibre helps you slim; and we should be eating at least 30 grams a day of it. Fibre is unrefined carbohydrate. It is a complex carbohydrate and consists of starches and fibre bound up together in such things as bread, potatoes, fruit, vegetables, nuts and pulses.

Fibre is important to us in healthy eating because it provides filling food without being fattening. Bulky carbohydrates satisfy our hunger with less than half the calories weight for weight of fatty food: 1 gram of carbohydrate is 4 calories; 1 gram of fat is 9 calories.

There are two types of fibre – soluble and insoluble. Insoluble fibre is found in cereals and in fibrous fruit and vegetables. This fibre, or roughage, helps food and waste products to pass through the digestive system. Food containing insoluble fibre is satisfying as it needs more chewing than other foods and, as it absorbs water and swells in the stomach, it is filling.

Soluble fibre, found in fruit, vegetables and pulses, helps prevent hunger between meals, as it delays the absorption of certain nutrients. Without this fibre, there can be a large fall in the blood sugar level, which causes hunger. Oat bran, which is the outer protective coating of the oat grain, is one of the best sources of soluble fibre and can be eaten raw or cooked.

The Fat and Fibre Counter later in the book lists the fibre in all the major foods but the following lists give a general idea of high and low fibre contents in some of the main foods:

HIGH

Peas   Bran   Prunes   Beans
Sweetcorn   Bananas   Wholemeal
bread   Brown rice   Dried fruit
Potatoes, baked   Leafy vegetables

MEDIUM

Most green vegetables   Most nuts
Apples   Oranges   Celery

LOW

Potatoes, boiled   White bread
White rice   Tomatoes   Lettuce
Cucumber   Grapefruit

NONE

Meat   Fish   Eggs   Sugar
Milk   Butter   Cheese

● REDUCE SALT

We eat up to ten times the amount of salt we actually need; on average about two teaspoonfuls a day, half of which is added by manufacturers during food processing.

Too much salt can cause high blood pressure, which can increase the risk of heart disease. If you eat a balanced diet you will get all the salt you need without having to add it to your diet. Try reducing your use of salt slowly over a period of weeks and use flavouring substitutes like herbs, spices and lemon juice. Try to break the habit of adding salt at the table, if necessary using a low sodium salt substitute. And cut down on crisps, salted meat, salted fish and processed canned foods.

A WAY OF LIFE

In a recent survey carried out for *New Woman* magazine, 500 women aged between 20 and 45 were asked about their personal experiences of losing weight. The majority claimed that the best method for them was simply cutting down on fattening foods, and following healthy eating habits. The report concluded that 'all the evidence is that while a gradual change in eating patterns may yield slower results, those results are far more likely to prove permanent'.

The Walking Diet is not a short term cure. It is a long term solution to fitness and health. Walking makes you slim, builds cardiovascular fitness, and can develop into a long term habit that you can use for the rest of your life. And your own personal 'diata' will help you to build up the long term eating habits that are necessary for good health.

We have suggested that 'diata' means a way of living; it means taking a holistic viewpoint on the food we eat and the exercise our bodies need. It means taking into account our current eating habits and including in our diet the necessary changes that are required to maintain a healthy lifestyle.

Don't let anyone tell you that diet and exercise don't go together. THEY DO. A balanced healthy approach to lifestyle (your own personal 'diata') is a balance between healthy eating, exercise and relaxation.

AND DON'T FORGET! Homo sedentarius is most of us: your spouse perhaps, your father, Uncle Fred, the family next door, the girl sitting all day behind the reception desk at work.

Don't become next year's statistics. Switch off the television set, follow the recipes, get out and walk, and just LET GO. Remember, your health is in your own hands; or should that be feet?

CHAPTER 3

WALKING MAKES YOU SLIM

If you do not get active and stay active, you've got a snowball's chance in hell of maintaining any weight loss. You will face semi-starvation for the rest of your life if you remain sedentary and want to control your weight.
MARTIN KATAHN — *THE ROTATION DIET*

Millions of people have already discovered the magic of walking and are walking regularly for fitness, slimness and health. Why cause ourselves so much anxiety, and spend so much time, money and energy on failed diet/exercise routines when the answer to all our problems is staring us right in the face.

Walking is the easiest, cheapest, most convenient, most effective (in the long term) exercise of all. And we have been doing it all our lives. The only problem is that we are not doing enough of it and in the right way.

To begin with we already have a solid foundation from which to build our exercise programme. We all walk a certain amount every day of our lives, even if we are sedentary, and that is easier than starting from scratch for the first time jogging or cycling.

Our bodies already use the muscles required to walk, so it is simply a question of increasing the duration and then the intensity of our walking in order to build up to the fitness level that we require.

But it is still boring old walking, isn't it?

No, it isn't.

Forget about strolling down to the shops to get a newspaper or sauntering in the park with the family on Sundays. For that is exactly what it is, strolling and sauntering. There is nothing wrong with that. Both activities can be very enjoyable. But neither activity will get you very far in your quest for fitness, and to be honest they give walking a bad name.

Brisk fitness walking – aerobic walking – is an exhilarating experience. Aerobic walking provides all the fitness benefits of jogging, cycling and rowing with less chance of injury, 'burn-out' and sheer boredom. And it really does make you slim.

HOW IT WORKS

There was a time when diet books insisted that exercise could not help in losing weight. But these days most people would agree that regular whole body continuous exercise, such as brisk fitness walking, is an effective way of losing weight, particularly fat.

And it works for several reasons:

1. IT'S AEROBIC – The key to walking aerobically is to walk at a pace of 3·5–4·0 miles per hour for a minimum of 20 minutes, during which time the heart rate is elevated to 60–85 per cent of its

maximum. Below 60 per cent the exercise will not have an aerobic effect and only very fit people can gain any aerobic effect above the 85 per cent level (see Table 3).

TABLE 3

Age	Maximum Heart Rate	60% Level	85% Level
20	200	120	170
25	195	117	166
30	190	114	162
35	185	111	157
40	180	108	153
45	175	105	149
50	170	102	145
55	165	99	140
60	160	96	136
65	155	93	132
70	150	90	128

If you think about it, air is essentially the 'breath of life'. We cannot live without it, but many of us are living each day with too little of it. Our sedentary lifestyle induces shallow breathing and instead of inhaling as much as 3,000 cubic centimetres of air, we often inhale as little as 500 cubic centimetres. Imagine what the performance of your motor car would be like if you reduced the air supply to the carburettor. It would jump and shudder and you would have a very uncomfortable ride. Lack of sufficient oxygen affects our bodies in the same way. We feel tired and sluggish and cannot be bothered to do anything. We are trying to run our bodies on too little air.

Aerobic means literally 'with oxygen' and walking aerobically causes the lungs to take in more air with less effort. The lungs are then able to extract more oxygen from the increased air supply and deliver it to the cells where it is needed to combine with food to produce energy.

It is this increase in oxygen that provides the extra fuel to burn up the food in our internal fire. When oxygen is supplied to a flame it burns faster; the same thing happens to our body when we walk aerobically. The action of the lungs works like a bellows which enriches the internal fire where food is converted into energy. The result is an improvement in the vital efficiency of the lungs and the whole cardiovascular (CV) system.

As the CV system improves, the blood vessels enlarge and become more elastic, and the heart becomes bigger and stronger. The muscles are strengthened by an increased flow of blood, as are the ligaments that attach them to the bones. Strength and mobility of joints improves, and because the muscles need more energy, stored body fat is broken down and utilised, leading to a reduction in weight.

It is the heart and lungs that help to determine the fitness of the whole body. Other organs, although vital in their own way, cannot survive without a blood supply rich in oxygen and nutrients. Whenever you run for a train, cope with stress at work, or lose your temper, the heart and lungs have to cope with the extra demands placed on them. Your heart beats faster; your lungs take in more air. And it is the healthy CV system that can cope easily with all the strains placed upon it by modern living. Conversely, it is the weak CV system that is easy prey to high blood pressure, coronary attack, colds, viruses, and other diseases. Listen to what Gabe Mirkin and Martshall Hoffmann in *The Sportsmedicine Book* say about the athlete's heart:

Because the athlete's heart is so muscular it can pump the same amount of blood with 50 beats per minute that the average heart pumps with 75 beats. Thus the athlete's heart will beat 13 million fewer times per year. It works less, rests more, and consequently takes a much longer time to wear out.

You may not end up with an athlete's heart through aerobic walking, but you will have gone a long way to improving its strength and efficiency, thus ensuring a longer and healthier life.

You should now be able to see that aerobic walking is vigorous sustained exercise that provides all the health and fitness benefits of jogging, cycling and rowing. And it is this regular aerobic routine that speeds up the body by increasing its metabolic rate and gives it the ability to shed those extra pounds.

2. IT INCREASES YOUR METABOLIC RATE

– Aerobic exercise such as brisk walking speeds up your metabolic rate. Basal or resting metabolic rate (BMR) is the speed your body burns calories at rest – in other words carrying out the job of staying alive: blood circulation, cell growth, digestion, thinking and so on.

The BMR of a man or woman is dependent on weight, height, fitness and body composition. Body composition is the amount of lean muscle compared with fat. A fat 60 kilogram person will have less lean tissue in total body mass than a thin 60 kilogram person, the difference being the excess fat.

A person's total daily need for calories is the amount of calories needed to maintain BMR plus the calories needed for movement, i.e. physical activity. Everyone's BMR is different. The important thing is that we can influence it through aerobic exercise.

The problem of dieting without increased physical activity is that the BMR slows down rather than speeds up. Then when you stop dieting, the body, which has been acting in a kind of starvation mode, finds that it has become used to its new BMR and requires less calories to function. And so it deposits the extra calories it does not need as fat. Dieting without exercise also forces the body to manage on less oxygen, and it reduces its oxygen intake even further when it has to take energy, not from food, but from the body itself.

In contrast, during aerobic walking the heart and respiratory rates increase and the BMR speeds up. It is the increase in oxygen and the increased BMR that burns off excess calories and keeps them off forever.

Generally speaking, compared with being sedentary (sitting watching TV, working at a desk), you will burn around three times more calories walking at 3 miles an hour. And when you walk aerobically at 4 miles an hour, you will burn around five times more calories than you would being sedentary.

Table 4 is an estimate of the calories you can expect to burn off as you increase your activity from a gentle stroll to brisk aerobic walking. It is based on a person weighing 150 pounds. These figures are only estimates because people have different metabolic rates. Men normally have higher BMRs than women because a larger part of their total body weight is muscle tissue, and muscle tissue can burn up to three times more energy than fat tissue, even when it is inactive.

Aerobic walking will help change your body composition by increasing the amount of muscle

TABLE 4

WALKING SPEED M.P.H.	PACE	CALORIES BURNED (APPROX)	
		IN 30 MIN	IN 1 HOUR
2	SLOW	120	240
2.5	MEDIUM	140	280
3	MEDIUM	160	320
3.5	BRISK	180	360
4	BRISK	210	420
4.5	FAST	250	500
WALKING UP MODERATE INCLINE	BRISK	300	600

tissue compared with fat tissue. This is important because up to half the weight normally lost on calorie-reducing diets without exercise is muscle tissue. And this loss of muscle tissue lowers BMR rather than increases it.

This is the problem of dieting without exercise. You can end up losing weight, lowering your BMR and be stuck with maintaining a semi-starvation diet to keep the pounds off. Regular aerobic walking, on the other hand, will increase your BMR and still allow you to eat well and stay healthy and slim.

Increased BMR is good news for aerobic walkers. For not only does it burn off on average up to 100 calories for every 15 minutes of activity, but the raised BMR can continue to burn off calories for several hours after exercising is over. And there is evidence to suggest that sustained aerobic walking not only increases BMR but that the increased BMR continues permanently.

3. IT SHEDS FAT – Most diets are calorie based and rely on calorie restriction for results. Until recently it had always been assumed that all calories are the same, regardless of where they came from. In other words a fat calorie was exactly the same as a carbohydrate or a protein calorie. And if we overate on any one of them then any surplus energy would end up by making us fat. However, recent research has confirmed that all calories are not the same.

Studies at Stanford University and the Human Nutrition Centre in Maryland, USA, have overturned the conventional wisdom. In one research study a group of overweight women were given a high fat diet while another group received a low fat diet. Both provided the same amount of calories. It was found that women on the high fat diet gained weight more easily than women on the low fat diet and a similar project for men reached the same conclusion.

The Vanderbilt Weight Management Program in the USA has produced similar results. Martin Katahn confirms that 'it's the fat in your diet that makes you fat . . . when it comes to being fat and overweight, it's primarily the fat calories that count, not the carbohydrate and protein calories' (*T-Factor Diet*).

In the typical Western diet all the energy in protein is burned up daily and none is converted and stored as fat. And whereas protein and carbohydrates use 25 per cent of energy converting dietary fat to body fat, fat itself requires very little energy to convert dietary fat to body fat – 3 per cent in fact. It is the ease with which the body converts dietary fat to body fat that causes the main problem in weight control. It is not just weight control that we need but fat control.

Although the body is not as efficient at converting excess carbohydrate to body fat as it is at converting dietary fat to body fat, it was thought until recently that any extra calories would still end up as body fat. This has now been disproved. Under most circumstances the body converts very little carbohydrate to body fat. Our bodies are designed to burn carbohydrates and store fats.

And this is where metabolic rate (BMR) comes in again. Because if you eat a regular high carbohydrate diet then your BMR is likely to be higher than a person eating a high fat diet. Your body has to work that much harder to convert the additional carbohydrate into energy and it is this thermic effect which can burn off up to another 200–300 calories each day. And remember that this is in addition to the calories you are burning away every day during aerobic walking, another 200–400 calories depending upon time and effort.

The thermic effect (thermogenesis) is the action of the body in burning up excess calories consumed as food energy to produce heat. The additional thermic effect produced by the Walking Diet (low fat food and aerobic exercise) will gradually help produce the change in body shape that you desire and bring you back to your target weight.

As we know, exercise plays an important part in any diet/exercise routine, but the key thing is that all exercise is not the same. Aerobic walking carried out as part of the Walking Diet will burn off more fat during the activity period than carbohydrate. Not only will you burn off up to 300 calories walking briskly at 4 miles an hour for 45 minutes, but up to 180 of these calories will be fat calories.

In contrast, if you perform an anaerobic (literally 'without air') activity such as squash for 45 minutes, then you will burn off up to 650 calories but only around 260 of these will be fat calories. This is because regular continuous aerobic exercise like brisk walking is a fat burning activity whereas start-stop anaerobic exercises like squash and tennis are carbohydrate burning activities.

During aerobic walking your heart and breathing rates increase, level out, then remain there for the duration of the exercise. Your body is supplied with the oxygen it needs when it needs it to burn in its fuel mixture. Anaerobic exercise on the other hand requires short sudden bursts of energy which are provided by fuel supplied from the muscles, and not from the increased oxygen supply provided by aerobic exercise. This leads to the feeling of rapid heart beat and breathlessness that is typical of anaerobic exercise.

The good news for everyone is that aerobic walking has the greatest effect around the hips and thighs where fat tends to accumulate, particularly in women. This is good news for all women who have been unsuccessful with hip and thigh diets that concentrate mainly on dieting and calorie-counting. It's also good news for men who are trying to lose weight around their hips and thighs and especially their waistlines. Regular aerobic activity not only burns off this excess fat, but it keeps it off forever.

I hope you are now convinced that regular aerobic walking is the answer to all your exercise and diet needs and that you cannot wait to get out and try it. As the saying goes, the journey of a thousand miles begins with just one step, so by now you should be thinking of putting all your good intentions into practice and getting out to walk.

STARTING OUT

This walk is the beginning of a habit which will change the rest of your life. So put on suitable clothing and a pair of comfortable sturdy shoes and set yourself a target of a 20 minute brisk invigorating walk.

You can walk almost anywhere that is convenient and safe, but we have found that the easiest and quickest way to build a regular walking habit is to walk right out our own front door and do a circuit around the block and back again. Once you start walking regularly you can vary your walks by going to the park, the beach or the hills. But in the beginning you should make it as easy as possible to get into the habit without excuses getting in the way. The aim is to start walking and keep walking.

But first a HEALTH WARNING!

If you are uncertain about your physical condition; if you are overweight, suffer from cardiovascular or respiratory disease, or have a medically diagnosed problem, then you should consult your doctor before starting to walk briskly. And beware of the passive fitness syndrome. Just because you are thin and never suffer a day's illness does not mean that you can embark on an energetic walking programme without building up to it. The advice is always the same. Warm up first (follow the exercises in Chapter 6 – The Walker's Workout), start slowly and don't hurt yourself, for that is the fastest way to break the routine in your programme and is often the reason why so many exercise programmes fail.

The resting pulse rate (heart rate) is a rough guide to your general physical condition. It is a barometer which determines your state of wellbeing, stress or illness. It should be taken first thing in the morning, before it has had time to be increased by exertion, mental excitement, eating, or stimulants like tea, coffee or nicotine.

Take your resting pulse rate by first sitting quietly in a chair and breathing normally. Then use either of the following methods:

1. Place the first two fingers of your right hand on the main artery of the inner wrist of your left hand just below the base of the thumb. Count the number of beats in either 15 or 30 seconds and multiply by either four or two to obtain the resting pulse rate.

2. Place two fingers on your neck beside your windpipe; you will feel the pulse. This is the

carotid artery which carries blood to the head. Count the number of beats in the same way as for the wrist. Whatever you do, don't press both sides of the neck at the same time: you could diminish the flow of blood to the head, or even cut it off.

Your pulse rate changes throughout the day. It is lowest whilst sleeping. On awakening it will rise from five to ten beats a minute, and during the day it will rise gradually and may be up to ten beats higher at bedtime than it was when you got up in the morning.

Pulse rates vary greatly. Generally speaking, the lower the resting pulse rate, the healthier you are. The average for men is between 70 and 85 a minute; a woman's pulse tends to be faster at 75–90 beats a minute. If your pulse rate is between 90 and 100, it is likely that you are unfit, and a brisk walking routine will gradually bring it down. Having said that, some people have normal pulse rates up to 100 and some athletes and other normal people have pulse rates as low as 40. The main thing to remember is that the heart is simply a pump: the less work it has to do (the less beats it makes), the longer it is going to last.

You should now begin your walking routine to suit your physical condition. If you have been sedentary for some time and are not used to physical exertion, then you should begin slowly, walking for no more than 20 minutes every other day, at a pace which stretches you but does not overtire you. Your goal should be to exert yourself a little more each time until you reach a brisk pace and you feel comfortable with it. On alternate days walk at a slower pace to help you build up a regular habit of walking. Then continue walking at this pace until you feel ready to go on to the 30 day walk back to fitness programme later in this chapter.

Whatever you do don't hurt yourself. It is at the beginning of an exercise routine, when the desire for results exceeds the ability to cope, that you will suffer from musculo-skeletal injuries. It's at this point that so many people give up. The beauty of walking is that no matter where you start, you can gradually build up the duration and intensity of your routine until you reach the fitness level that you require.

If you are already physically active, then you should start out with a brisk, vigorous walk for 20 minutes, stretching yourself as you walk. At the end of it you should feel refreshed. If you feel tired then you are going too fast. If you cannot hold a conversation with someone without getting out of breath then you are going too fast. The key to the whole thing is to listen to what your body is telling you and to slow down if necessary. You should walk briskly every other day, and on alternate days walk for 20 minutes at a slower pace to build up a regular routine, until you feel ready to go on to the 30-day walk back to fitness programme at the end of this chapter.

To get the real benefits of aerobic walking and to walk towards that fitter, slimmer you, then you have to achieve a walking heart rate between 60 per cent and 85 per cent of your maximum heart rate (refer again to Table 3).

There is a simple way of calculating your aerobic walking rate. Subtract your age from 220. This gives your maximum heart rate in beats per minute. Then multiply that figure by 0.60 (60 per cent) for the lower end of your aerobic walking rate and by 0.85 (85 per cent) for the higher end.

After you have been walking for about ten

minutes take your pulse. You will need a watch that records seconds for this. Take your pulse in the same way that you calculated your resting pulse rate earlier. If your heart is beating beyond the high end of your aerobic range then you are walking too fast. If you are unfit, three miles an hour will probably be a comfortable rate to walk at to reach your aerobic range.

When you first start out you should stick to the lower end of your aerobic range (60 per cent) until you feel comfortable with it. Then as you progress, measure your aerobic improvement by taking your pulse at several points during the walk and immediately upon finishing. This will ensure that you remain within your aerobic range.

As your fitness improves you will find that your heart rate decreases while performing the same level of exercise. This is because the increased size and strength of the heart muscle enables it to pump a larger volume of blood into the arteries with each beat.

Once you are comfortable walking at the 60 per cent level, then experiment up to the 70–75 per cent level. You should not need to go higher than this. At this level you should get all the fitness, slimness and cardiovascular benefits that you need.

But as you progress from the 60 per cent level upwards, remember that your body is the best judge of what feels comfortable. If it hurts then slow down. Gentle stretching is what is needed, not painful exertion. There is nothing more demoralising than coming home with an injury which keeps you out of action for a few weeks.

WALKING WITH THE WEATHER

You should keep up your walking routine regardless of the weather. There are few days when the weather is so unpleasant that it is impossible to walk; and even on a rainy day there are often periods when the rain stops. After all, the weather does not normally stop you getting to work, playing golf, or getting on with the rest of your life.

On a cold day you can keep your whole body warm with far less clothing than you may think. The main thing is to wear gloves, cover your head and neck, and keep your thighs warm. When the extremities are warm, the whole body can be kept warm with light clothing. If you start to feel too warm you can always take off the hat and gloves.

Don't put on too many sweaters. Instead, wear several light layers of clothing that can easily be added or removed as you walk. There are some excellent lightweight clothes available these days made from such materials as Gore-Tex, which keep out the wind and rain but allow your sweat to evaporate.

For warm-weather walking, wear light-coloured clothes to reflect the heat and light, and if it is sunny, wear a brimmed hat. Choose a time of day such as early morning, late afternoon, or early evening to walk.

Don't let the weather put you off. Once you build up a regular routine you will want to get outside whatever the weather is doing. And remember that you are walking for the psychological benefits as well as the fitness and slimness benefits. Each season has its own delights to offer. Mist and fog, snow, spring rain, and summer heat are all attractive and beautiful to the walker who takes the time to look.

FINDING YOUR STRIDE

Pace is the key to finding your stride and reaching a good rhythm in your walking. Set off at a good pace with the longest stride that is comfortable, letting your arms swing naturally in opposition to your feet.

The arms should move at the same speed as the legs. Relax your shoulders, then as you walk the arms will swing by themselves. When your right foot swings forward, your left arm will swing with it; when your left foot swings forward, your right arm will swing in opposition to it. The arms and shoulders move and swing in a pendulum motion in counterbalance to the legs and hips.

The legs and hips have the largest muscles in the body: let them set the rhythm, then let the arms follow that rhythm. You will notice that as your legs speed up so do your arms. Your elbows will bend naturally and you will feel the natural flow of brisk rhythmic walking.

With each stride you will begin to feel yourself reaching further with your hips. This is good news! The more you stretch your hips the more you will improve your shape. If you continue to stretch your hips forward, you will find that they move naturally without any sort of exaggerated wiggle.

You will now want to make sure that your feet are landing in the right place. The most comfortable and efficient way is to use the heel-toe method. The heel of your leading foot should touch the ground, just before the ball of the foot and toes. Then, as the heel touches the ground, lock your ankle and shift your weight forward with the knee bent, rocking forward onto the toes and using them to push you off to the next step.

WALKING TO YOUR GOAL WEIGHT

The first thing to do is to find a pair of old jeans or other piece of favourite clothing that is too tight and use this as a measure for making progress. There is nothing like the thrill a week or two later of being able to get back into clothing that you thought had been discarded forever.

Next, weigh yourself and make a note of it. If you don't know your height then measure that too. Then check yourself against the Height/Weight Chart (see Table 5). For each height there is an acceptable weight range covering small to large frames. If you are a woman your goal weight should be nearer the lower figure; for men, depending on build, it should be towards the higher end of the scale.

You now have a goal to aim for. But don't get obsessed with weight watching. Body weight fluctuates rapidly at times. Weigh yourself once a week and try to get back into your chosen piece of clothing. If you build up an aerobic walking programme you will soon see the excess pounds drop away and you will feel and look fitter and slimmer without weight watching.

By now you should have been out on several practice walks and determined your state of fitness. You should be listening carefully to what your body is telling you and you should be judging your pace and duration so that you finish tired and refreshed, not exhausted.

You are now ready to make some real progress. But don't look for instant results. Concentrate rather on the walking itself. Get into the habit first of feeling the sheer thrill and exhilaration of getting out of doors away from telephones, noise, and distractions. Think about how good you feel.

TABLE 5

HEIGHT/WEIGHT CHART			
Height without shoes ft in	Small frame st lb	Medium frame st lb	Large frame st lb
WOMEN			
4 10	7 2	7 12	8 7
4 11	7 4	8 0	8 10
5 0	7 7	8 2	8 13
5 1	7 10	8 5	9 2
5 2	7 13	8 7	9 5
5 3	8 2	8 10	9 8
5 4	8 6	9 0	9 12
5 5	8 10	9 5	10 2
5 6	9 0	9 10	10 6
5 7	9 4	10 0	10 10
5 8	9 8	10 5	11 0
5 9	9 12	10 10	11 5
5 10	10 3	11 2	11 10
MEN			
5 3	8 10	9 4	10 0
5 4	8 13	9 7	10 3
5 5	9 2	9 10	10 6
5 6	9 6	10 0	10 10
5 7	9 10	10 4	11 1
5 8	10 0	10 8	11 5
5 9	10 4	10 12	11 9
5 10	10 8	11 2	11 13
5 11	10 12	11 6	12 4
6 0	11 2	11 10	12 8
6 1	11 6	12 0	12 13
6 2	11 10	12 5	13 4
6 3	12 0	12 10	13 9

Tell yourself that this is a habit which is going to change your life forever, and that it is going to bring you the health, fitness and slimness that you deserve.

I promise you that if you persevere with aerobic walking the psychological benefits alone will make you want to get out every day. So let yourself go. You are learning to do the most natural thing in the world. This is what your body was designed for.

DISTANCE, TIME AND SPEED

As we have stressed previously, the easiest way to begin aerobic walking is to walk out of your own front door and do a circuit round the block and back, or around some other convenient route that is known to you. You will need to gauge the distances covered so the best way is to take a car ride around your proposed route and use the odometer to measure the distance between familiar landmarks. Alternatively, some bicycles have an odometer on them which you could use in the same way.

As you build up your walking program, you will need to increase the length of your circuit if you are going to cover several miles. And you will need to measure it. Or you can simply cover as many circuits as you want around the same track in the way that athletes do circuit training on a track. And you will want to calculate your speed.

It is useful to remember the following formulas:

1. Distance = Speed x Time
2. Speed = $\dfrac{\text{Distance}}{\text{Time}}$

3. Time = $\dfrac{\text{Distance}}{\text{Speed}}$

If you know any two of the above variables, it is easy to work out the third. Time is the easiest to measure: most people have a watch. So if you can measure the distance, it is then easy to calculate the speed.

Once you begin to stray from easily measured routes and landmarks, you will need to acquire a pedometer. A pedometer is a small gadget that clips onto your belt and you adjust it to the length of your own stride to measure the distance covered. With the help of your watch, it will also tell you the speed at which you are travelling. Pedometers can be purchased in most sports shops and large department stores.

There are two further methods to estimate the distance covered whilst walking:

1. WALKING SPEEDS (M.P.H.) – Walk for one mile along the route you have previously measured with the car's odometer and time yourself. If it took you 15 minutes then you were walking at 4 m.p.h.:

Speed = $\dfrac{\text{Distance}}{\text{Time}}$ = $\dfrac{1 \text{ mile}}{0.25 \text{ hours}}$

As you vary your walking pace (increase your speed), then repeat the above method to calculate your new walking speed. You will soon get a feel for the speed you walk at and be able to judge different walking paces (2.5, 3.0, 3.5, 4.0 m.p.h.). If you can estimate your speed, and you know the time, then it is easy to work out the distance:

Distance = Speed x Time

2. THE STEP METHOD – Count the number of steps that you take in one minute at your normal walking speed. Since the average stride is approximately two feet per step and there are 5,280 feet in one mile then it will take 2,640 steps to cover one mile. If your speed is 176 steps per minute then it will take 15 minutes to cover one mile:

$$
\begin{aligned}
\text{Distance} &= \text{Speed x Time} \\
&= 176 \text{ steps/min x 15 mins} \\
&= 2,640 \text{ steps}
\end{aligned}
$$

You may want to measure your exact stride in the way that a pedometer does. To do this, measure the distance from toe to toe or heel to heel when you take a normal stride. The easiest way is to get someone to help you. Then calculate the distance walked in the same way as above.

All this may sound very complicated. It is. The easiest way to measure distance is to get hold of a pedometer.

WALK BACK TO HEALTH & FITNESS IN 30 DAYS

At the same time as you begin your 30 day walking programme, you should also begin the 30 day Walking Diet as detailed in Chapter 4. You should be aiming to lose 1–2 lbs per week until you get back to your goal weight. This is quite enough to lose, and it is the most efficient way to control weight loss. It is quite normal of course to have a rapid weight loss of several pounds in the first week due mainly to water loss (our bodies are 70 per cent water).

Although the walking programme and the diet routine are organised through Day 1 to 30, we recommend that you begin the programme on a Monday, as the aerobic walking gradually builds up throughout the week, with more aerobic walking on weekends.

Before you walk, always warm up first (using the warm-up exercises in Chapter 6 – The Walker's Workout). Then start slowly, and build up your speed as you go along.

As this chapter proceeds, there is an aerobic walking record for you to fill in. If you wish, you can copy this and use it as an ongoing walking record after the 30 days. The record will help to measure your progress and to motivate you; for it is motivation that will get you going, and it is motivation that will keep you going. If you keep this up to date, then you can plan each day or week in advance, inserting where, when and for how long you are going to walk. You will notice that each day is divided into a.m. and p.m. Some days you may not be able to fit in your daily walk in one session, so you can divide it into an a.m. and a p.m. session. However, we do not recommend that you split the times for your aerobic walks during the first 14 days. Walk for 20 or 30 minutes aerobically, as directed, during this time, either a.m. or p.m. Then, if you wish, split your walks into a.m. and p.m. on alternate days when you are walking at a moderate pace.

The times suggested throughout the 30 day programme are minimum times that you should walk each day. If you hit your stride and get a rhythm going, you may feel comfortable going on a little longer than the minimum times. If it feels good, then stretch a little further before finishing. Then as you walk each day you can compare your actual, achieved time against your planned time; and you can record the distance, speed and any other information about the route (whether it is flat, rough ground, or uphill). At the end of each week you can then add up your total time and compare your planned and achieved time to measure your progress; and you can do the same thing at the end of 30 days.

Please don't treat your walking record as a chore to fill in every day. Be businesslike about it. Clearly defined aims and objectives will bring you the results you desire, and remember: if you don't know where you are going, then how are you going to know when you have got there.

WEEK 1

DAY 1 – Begin by walking aerobically (3.5 – 4.0 m.p.h.) for 20 minutes around the route you have measured out. Set off at a good pace, with the longest stride that is comfortable, your arms swinging naturally in opposition to your legs. Remember to take your pulse at intervals along the walk to make sure you are within your aerobic range.

DAY 2 – Walk for 20 minutes at a moderate pace and simply take in the joy of walking. For the first three weeks you will be alternating aerobic walking with moderate walking for the first four days each week, followed by one day's rest. This will help you get into the habit of regular walking without placing too much emphasis initially on results.

DAY 3 – Walk aerobically for 20 minutes. Concentrate on finding your stride and building a good rhythm.

DAY 4 – Walk for 20 minutes at a moderate pace.

You will now be feeling the psychological as well as the aerobic benefits of regular walking. You will not be able to wait to get out each day.

DAY 5 – Rest day.

DAY 6 – Walk aerobically for 20 minutes. As we have stressed, the times quoted are minimum times. Weekends are a good time to knock up those extra miles and get away from your measured route – into the country, etc.

DAY 7 – Repeat Day 6. At the end of the first week you will have a solid foundation on which to build in future weeks. You will already be feeling fitter, healthier, and be starting to shed the first few pounds of excess weight.

		Time Planned (Mins)	Time Walked (Mins)	Distance In Miles	Speed In M.p.h.	Route/Comment
DAY 1	A.M.					
	P.M.					
DAY 2	A.M.					
	P.M.					
DAY 3	A.M.					
	P.M.					
DAY 4	A.M.					
	P.M.					

		Time Planned (Mins)	Time Walked (Mins)	Distance In Miles	Speed In M.p.h.	Route/Comment
DAY 5	A.M.					
	P.M.					
DAY 6	A.M.					
	P.M.					
DAY 7	A.M.					
	P.M.					
WEEKLY TOTALS					Av. Speed	

WEEK 2

DAY 8 – You are now starting to make progress, and can increase your walking time from 20 to 30 minutes each day. The important thing is to increase time before pace; so walk at a moderate pace for 30 minutes, gently stretching yourself as you go.

DAY 9 – Walk aerobically for 30 minutes. It normally takes the first ten minutes of any brisk walk to get into a rhythm and feel aerobic, so increasing the time from 20 to 30 minutes is effectively doubling the aerobic benefits.

DAY 10 – Walk at a moderate pace for 30 minutes. Try early evening walks to de-stress after a hard day's work. Feel the rhythm in your feet, calves, thighs, arms and shoulders. Relax – and go with the flow.

DAY 11 – Walk aerobically for 30 minutes. Think about the calories you are burning up – 200 for every 30 minute walk!

DAY 12 – Rest day.

DAY 13 – Walk aerobically for 30 minutes. Remember that you are not only burning up calories while you walk, but your increased metabolic rate will keep burning up calories when you finish walking.

DAY 14 – Repeat Day 13.

		Time Planned (Mins)	Time Walked (Mins)	Distance In Miles	Speed In M.p.h.	Route/Comment
DAY 8	A.M.					
	P.M.					
DAY 9	A.M.					
	P.M.					
DAY 10	A.M.					
	P.M.					
DAY 11	A.M.					
	P.M.					

		Time Planned (Mins)	Time Walked (Mins)	Distance In Miles	Speed In M.p.h.	Route/Comment
DAY 12	A.M.					
	P.M.					
DAY 13	A.M.					
	P.M.					
DAY 14	A.M.					
	P.M.					
WEEKLY TOTALS					Av. Speed	

WEEK 3

DAY 15 – The cumulative benefits of regular walking will now be starting to add up and you will be well on your way to that healthier, slimmer you. You can now increase your walking time from 30 minutes to 45 minutes per day: walk at a moderate pace for 45 minutes. Take your spouse, a friend, or the children for a walk.

DAY 16 – Walk aerobically for 45 minutes. If you wish, split your walking time between a.m and p.m. You can now start venturing away from your measured route and start looking for additional ways to clock up the extra miles – try walking to the shops instead of driving; try parking the car further away from work and walking the rest of the way; or getting off the bus or train one or two stops from your destination and walking the rest of the way.

DAY 17 – Walk at a moderate pace for 45 minutes. Think of all the opportunities that are available each day to walk, instead of taking the easy option by using cars, buses, taxis and trains. The miles all add up.

DAY 18 – Walk aerobically for 45 minutes. In your aerobic walking record we mentioned that you should make a note of conditions about the route. This is important because walking uphill requires more energy than walking along a level surface. Uphill walking is a great calorie burner (up to 600 calories an hour); even rough road surfaces help to burn off more calories. Try small hills first.

DAY 19 – Rest day.

DAY 20 – Walk aerobically for 45 minutes. Try energy breathing as you walk: breathe in through the nostrils counting 1 to 8 then out through the mouth counting 1 to 8.

DAY 21 – Repeat Day 20.

	Time Planned (Mins)	Time Walked (Mins)	Distance In Miles	Speed In M.p.h.	Route/Comment
DAY 15 A.M.					
P.M.					
DAY 16 A.M.					
P.M.					
DAY 17 A.M.					
P.M.					
DAY 18 A.M.					
P.M.					

		Time Planned (Mins)	Time Walked (Mins)	Distance In Miles	Speed In M.p.h.	Route/Comment
DAY 19	A.M.					
	P.M.					
DAY 20	A.M.					
	P.M.					
DAY 21	A.M.					
	P.M.					
WEEKLY TOTALS					Av. Speed	

WEEK 4

DAY 22 – Only nine more days to go. Today, walk at a moderate pace for 45 minutes. Vary your walking routine with morning walks, lunchtime walks, late afternoon walks, early evening walks. Try walking breaks instead of coffee breaks. The miles all add up.

DAY 23 – Walk aerobically for 45 minutes. Over the past week you have been walking away a minimum of 300 calories a day during your walk, and your increased metabolic rate will have been burning up another few hundred calories when you have finished walking. And all this is in addition to the calories you will be shedding by using the low fat recipes in the Walking Diet.

DAY 24 – Walk aerobically for 45 minutes. See the world at 4 miles an hour; this is what your body was designed for.

DAY 25 – Repeat Day 24. Cultivate awareness: savour the sights and sounds of the journey. Walk to break out of the pattern and routine of normal daily living.

DAY 26 – Rest day.

DAY 27 – Walk aerobically for 45 minutes. Try inner walking and walking meditation (see Chapter 8). Discover who you are. Walk for the inner benefits as well as the fitness and slimness benefits.

DAY 28 – Repeat Day 27.

DAY 29 – Almost there! Only two days left. Walk aerobically today for 45 minutes. After four weeks of aerobic workouts, you

have built the foundations for a lifetime's health
and fitness.

DAY 30 – The final day: walk aerobically for 45
minutes. Feel the wind in your hair, and
the satisfaction of a task well done. In
the past 30 days you have been training
your body to work at its optimum
potential; and you will now have a good
idea of what you can achieve by using
the Walking Diet recipes and aerobic
walking. Keep walking!

It may take longer than 30 days to achieve your
goal weight; it depends how much you need to
lose. But when you do achieve it, you will find
that you can then use aerobic walking as part of
an ongoing maintenance programme to keep you
at your goal weight. In future you will be in control
of your own body.

Once you have reached your goal weight, you
will want to maintain the health, fitness and slimness benefits that you have achieved. You should
continue to walk aerobically for a minimum of 30
minutes each day, four times a week; and you
should continue to use the low fat Walking Diet
recipes and adapt them to your own diet.

Everyone binges on food from time to time,
particularly at Christmas and holiday periods, but
you will find that once aerobic walking becomes
an enjoyable habit, it will be easy to walk away
those excess pounds any time you need to. You
simply use the Walking Diet, put your foot down,
and clock up the necessary aerobic miles to get you
back to your goal weight.

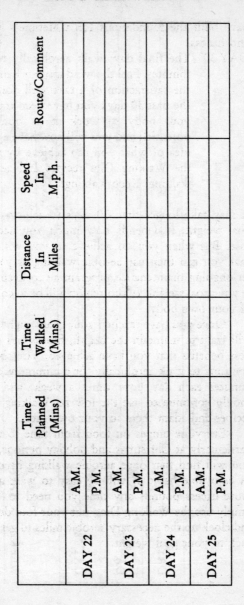

		Time Planned (Mins)	Time Walked (Mins)	Distance In Miles	Speed In M.p.h.	Route/Comment
DAY 22	A.M.					
	P.M.					
DAY 23	A.M.					
	P.M.					
DAY 24	A.M.					
	P.M.					
DAY 25	A.M.					
	P.M.					

		Time Planned (Mins)	Time Walked (Mins)	Distance In Miles	Speed In M.p.h.	Route/Comment
DAY 26	A.M.					
	P.M.					
DAY 27	A.M.					
	P.M.					
DAY 28	A.M.					
	P.M.					
					Av. Speed	
WEEKLY TOTALS						

		Time Planned (Mins)	Time Walked (Mins)	Distance In Miles	Speed In M.p.h.	Route/Comment
DAY 29	A.M.					
	P.M.					
DAY 30	A.M.					
	P.M.					
MONTHLY TOTALS					Av. Speed	

CHAPTER 4

THE WALKING DIET

'Will you walk a little faster?'
said a whiting to a snail
LEWIS CARROLL

The recipes in the Walking Diet are easy to follow and quickly prepared, so that even the busiest people have a chance to cook mouth-watering food that is full of goodness and at the same time is low in fat.

Having formed the habit of buying lots of fresh fruit and vegetables, fish, white meat and low fat alternatives to dairy products, we need to cook interesting and attractively presented dishes. This is not difficult, even for an inexperienced cook. The recipes are very versatile. In many cases, you can change the meat or fish suggested, to make an equally tasty dish. For instance, Swordfish Pilaki could easily be made with halibut or cod and the Tuna Tortiglioni could be made with any other fish or indeed some ham cut into pieces. Use smoked mackerel, smoked trout or kippers instead of smoked salmon to make a pâté and use other vegetables for the kebabs.

When shopping, see which are the best foods available. Many of the most highly regarded chefs choose their menus after seeing for themselves which the freshest foods are at the market!

If it is more convenient to prepare, for instance, Day 5's recipes on Day 3, then do so, as long as within the week you are eating a balance of meat, fish, vegetables and fruit. Some people prefer to eat their main meal at lunchtime and their light meal in the evening, whereas for others it is more practical to do the reverse. Therefore, adapt the diet according to your lifestyle, to your personal diata.

The diet is laid out in such a way that, starting on a Monday, the slightly more elaborate meals are at the weekend. If you wish to start on another day, by all means do so; simply change the order within the week if you so wish.

Bearing in mind that many people eat lunch at work, most of the light meal dishes can be taken to work either in a food container or, for a more filling lunch, pocketed in some pitta bread.

Add more spices, herbs or garlic if this is to your taste. Adapt some of your own favourite recipes to low fat versions by using methods suggested in these recipes, such as cooking onions in water or in chopped tomatoes instead of frying them.

A meal should be an occasion enjoyed by all. Too many people nowadays seem to eat while watching television, hardly noticing what or how much they are eating. How much nicer for a family or friends or even just oneself to sit at a table set for a meal!

At the end of this chapter, there are suggestions for eating out and entertaining. If one is entertaining friends or business colleagues, it is nice to offer three courses, but this does not have to be the case every day. When eating on your own or with the family, serve a variety of crudités (raw vegetables) soaked in lemon juice or with a little

Day	Light Meal	Main Meal
1	Greek Salad	Salmon Risotto
2	Smoked Mackerel & Red Kidney Bean Salad	Aubergine à l'Italienne
3	Shredded Ham & Grape Pitta/Open Sandwich	Spaghetti alle Vongole
4	Watercress & Kiwi Fruit Salad	Tortilla
5	Stuffed Peppers	Royal Indian Chicken
6	Jacket Potato with Chilli Beans	Swordfish Pilaki
7	Salade Niçoise	Turkey Provençal
8	Potato & Herring Salad	Mushrooms à la Grecque
9	Beetroot & Chicory Salad	Penne with Ham
10	Sweetcorn & Red Pepper Mayonnaise	Mackerel in Orange dressing
11	Waldorf Pitta/Open Sandwich	Leeks Mornay
12	Pasta Salad	Chinese Pork Fillet, Prawns & Celery
13	Jacket Potato with Cottage Cheese & Kiwi Fruit	Gigot of Monkfish
14	Fennel & Smoked Trout Salad	Chicken Lombattini
15	Lentil & Tomato Salad	Tagliatelle with Prawns

16	Courgettes & Mushrooms with Rice	Magyar Goulash
17	Salmon & Apple Mayonnaise	Mushroom Risotto
18	Tabbouleh	Sardines Provençales
19	Chicory, Orange & Cucumber Pitta/Open Sandwich	Jambalaya
20	Jacket Potato with Herring	Mediterranean Vegetables
21	Soya Bean Casserole	Venison with Black Cherries
22	Feta & Bacon Salad	Fennel Provençal
23	Mangetout, Tomato & Cashew Nut Salad	Saumon aux Epinards
24	Broad Bean & Ham Mayonnaise	Lamb Koftas
25	Spinach, Cottage Cheese and Pear Salad	Tuna Tortiglioni
26	Crab & Watercress Pitta/Open Sandwich	Aubergine & Courgette Kebabs
27	Jacket Potato with Tuna Mayonnaise	Chicken & Seafood Paella
28	Marinated Herrings	Mexican Beef
29	Pasta & Pepper Salad	Sweetcorn Mornay
30	Prawn & Rice Shells	Chicken In Mint & Yogurt Marinade

reduced calorie mayonnaise as a dip. Thin strips of carrot, celery, cucumber and pepper, cauliflower florets and chicory leaves are all excellent foods, taste good and look appetising. Generally, eat fresh fruit or yogurt as a dessert. Take advantage of the enormous variety of fruit now to be found in the shops. Whatever the circumstances, always present the food in an attractive way!

RECIPES

All recipes are for two people. Simply halve or multiply quantities as required.

DAY 1 – GREEK SALAD

---

crispy lettuce leaves (Iceberg or Cos)
1 beef tomato, cut into wedges
cucumber, cut into wedges
raw onion rings (soaked in cold water for half an hour if possible)
75 g (3 oz) Feta cheese
8 black olives
2 lemon wedges
lemon juice
freshly ground pepper

Arrange salad, squeeze over some lemon juice and add freshly ground pepper. Garnish with lemon wedges and serve with pitta bread.

SALMON RISOTTO

---

150 g (6 oz) boneless fresh salmon
1 medium onion, chopped
½ fennel, chopped
1 small tin sweetcorn, drained
100 g (4 oz) frozen petits pois

300 ml (10 fl oz) fish stock
75 ml (3 fl oz) white wine
75 ml (3 fl oz) water
3 ml (½ tsp) Nam Pla fish sauce
  (available from Oriental delicatessens)
freshly ground pepper and salt
100 g (4 oz) risotto rice
5 ml (1 tsp) sunflower oil
2 wedges of lime

Poach the salmon in the white wine and water for 5
minutes. Remove the salmon. Cook the fennel, onion
and petits pois gently in the cooking liquid for 10
minutes, then put with the salmon, reserving the cooking juices. Add the fish stock to the juices and keep
warm. In another pan, warm the sunflower oil. Add the
Risotto rice and, stirring continuously, cook for 2–3
minutes. Add 150 ml (6 fl oz) of the stock to the rice
and simmer, stirring occasionally, until the liquid is
absorbed. Add a further 150 ml of the stock, repeating
the process. Finally, add the rest of the stock and the
salt and pepper. If the rice is still not cooked, add a
small amount of water. Stir in the Nam Pla fish sauce,
sweetcorn, petits pois, fennel and onion and finally, for
a few moments, the salmon. Garnish with wedges of
lime.

DAY 2 – SMOKED MACKEREL AND RED KIDNEY BEAN SALAD

---

1 large smoked mackerel, skinned and flaked
1 small tin red kidney beans, drained
1 small onion, finely chopped
lemon juice
freshly ground pepper
4 chicory leaves

Mix the smoked mackerel, red kidney beans and onion
together. Squeeze over some lemon juice and add freshly

ground pepper. Garnish with chicory leaves cut into rings. Serve with a wedge of fresh wholemeal bread.

AUBERGINE A L'ITALIENNE

1 large aubergine
1 medium onion
1 small tin tomatoes
1 medium red pepper
100 g (4 oz) mushrooms
1 Mozzarella cheese
10 g (2 tsp) grated Parmesan cheese
10 g (2 tsp) chopped fresh basil
  or 5g (1 tsp) dried mixed herbs
1 clove garlic, chopped
5 ml (1 tsp) Nam Pla fish sauce
freshly ground pepper and salt

Slice the aubergines into ⅓" rings and chop onion. Cook together in boiling, salted water for 10 minutes. Drain and arrange in an ovenproof dish. Chop the red pepper and mushrooms and arrange on the aubergines. Pour the tomatoes over the vegetables. Add the garlic, herbs, Nam Pla fish sauce, salt and pepper. Slice the Mozzarella cheese fairly thinly and arrange on the vegetables. Sprinkle the Parmesan cheese over the top. Bake in a preheated oven, Gas Mark 6, (200C/400F), for 30 minutes. Put under a hot grill for a few moments until golden. Serve with crusty brown bread.

DAY 3 – SHREDDED HAM AND GRAPE PITTA / OPEN SANDWICH

75 g (3 oz) lean cooked ham, shredded
75 g (3 oz) grapes, halved and seeded
6 capers, chopped
10 ml (2 tsp) reduced calorie mayonnaise
freshly ground pepper

Mix all ingredients together and pile into a wholemeal pitta or onto a slice of fresh wholemeal bread.

SPAGHETTI ALLE VONGOLE

1 tin baby clams
1 medium onion, chopped
100 g (4 oz) frozen petits pois
50 g (2 oz) mushrooms, sliced
1 tin chopped tomatoes
1 clove garlic, chopped
5 ml (1 tsp) chopped fresh parsley
   or 3 ml (½ tsp) dried mixed herbs
5 ml (1 tsp) tomato purée
75 ml (3 fl oz) white wine or water
5 ml (1 tsp) Nam Pla fish sauce
freshly ground pepper and salt
spaghetti (wholewheat) cooked as directed
2 wedges of lemon

Cook the onion, garlic and petits pois in the tomatoes for 10 minutes. Add the mushrooms, herbs, tomato purée, wine or water, fish sauce and salt and pepper. Finally, add the clams. Serve the spaghetti with the clam sauce poured over. Garnish with wedges of lemon.

DAY 4 – WATERCRESS AND KIWI FRUIT SALAD

watercress
2 kiwi fruit, peeled and cut into pieces
cucumber, cut into small pieces
6 radishes, sliced
6 cashews, chopped
5 ml (1 tsp) reduced calorie mayonnaise
10 ml (2 tsp) low fat natural yogurt
freshly ground black pepper

Mix salad ingredients together. Combine mayonnaise and yogurt and mix with salad. Scatter over the chopped cashews and add some freshly ground black pepper.

TORTILLA

1 medium onion
1 red pepper
2 medium potatoes, peeled, cut into ⅓″ slices and boiled
3 ml (½ tsp) dried mixed herbs
5 ml (1 tsp) sunflower oil
3 eggs
freshly ground pepper and salt

Cook the chopped onion and red pepper in the sunflower oil in a non-stick frying pan. Add the cooked potato slices and the herbs. Whisk the eggs with a little water and some salt and pepper and pour over the vegetables. Cook until the tortilla is set. Serve with a green salad.

DAY 5 – STUFFED PEPPERS

1 medium green pepper (cut in half lengthways
1 medium red pepper   and de-seeded)
1 medium onion, chopped
1 clove garlic, chopped
75 g (3 oz) brown rice, cooked
1 small tin tomatoes
5 ml (1 tsp) chopped fresh rosemary
  or 3 ml (½ tsp) dried mixed herbs
freshly ground black pepper

Simmer the onion and garlic in the tomatoes, herbs and black pepper. Remove the vegetables from the liquid and mix with the rice. Arrange the rice and vegetable mixture into the pepper halves. Put in an ovenproof dish. Make the cooking liquid up to 250 ml with water and pour over the peppers. Cover the dish and bake in a preheated oven, Gas Mark 5 (190C/375F) for 30 minutes.

ROYAL INDIAN CHICKEN

2 chicken breast fillets
1 medium onion
100 g (4 oz) mushrooms, chopped
50 g (2 oz) ground almonds
125 g (5 oz) low-fat natural yogurt
10 ml (2 tsp) ground coriander
5 ml (1 tsp) ground cumin
3 ml (½ tsp) ground turmeric
3 ml (½ tsp) hot chilli powder
10 ml (2 tsp) lemon juice
200 ml (8 fl oz) water
freshly ground pepper and salt
toasted almonds

Cut the chicken into bite-size pieces and chop the onion. Poach gently in the water for 20 minutes. Add all other ingredients except the yogurt and toasted almonds. Stir carefully and cook for a further 10 minutes. Reduce liquid if necessary. Add the yogurt. Garnish the chicken with toasted almonds. Serve with brown rice.

DAY 6 – JACKET POTATO WITH CHILLI BEANS

2 large baking potatoes
1 large tin red kidney beans
10 ml (2 tsp) tomato purée
chilli sauce
lemon juice

Bake the potatoes. Heat the red kidney beans in the

mixture of tomato purée, chilli sauce and lemon juice. Open the jacket potatoes lengthways and pile the chilli beans on top.

SWORDFISH PILAKI

---

125 g (5 oz) swordfish (or any white fish), skin removed
1 small onion, chopped
1 clove garlic, chopped
small bunch celery leaves, chopped
150 g (6 oz) tomatoes, skinned and chopped
15 ml (1 tbsp) lemon juice
15 ml (1 tbsp) chopped fresh parsley
freshly ground pepper and salt
125 ml (5 fl oz) fish stock
4 green olives chopped

Simmer the onion, garlic, celery leaves and tomatoes in the fish stock for 10 minutes then add the swordfish. Cook gently for a further 10 minutes then break the fish into bite-size pieces. Reduce the liquid. Stir in the lemon juice and parsley and add salt and pepper to taste. Garnish with chopped green olives. Serve with brown rice and a tomato and onion salad.

DAY 7 – SALADE NICOISE

---

1 tin tuna in brine, drained
1 tin anchovy fillets, soaked in milk to reduce saltiness
1 hard-boiled egg, quartered
8 green or black olives
watercress or any other salad leaf
1 beef tomato
1 small green pepper
1 small onion
1 clove garlic

10 ml (2 tsp) lemon juice
5 ml (1 tsp) olive oil
freshly ground black pepper

Combine all salad ingredients with the flaked tuna. Toss
in the dressing of lemon juice and olive oil. Decorate
with the anchovy fillets, olives and quarters of hard-
boiled egg and finally grind some black pepper over the
salad.

TURKEY PROVENCAL

2 turkey breast fillets
1 small tin tomatoes
1 medium onion
100 g (4 oz) courgettes
50 g (2 oz) mushrooms
1 green or red pepper
50 g (2 oz) black olives
1 clove garlic
1 bouquet garni
  or 3 ml (½ tsp) dried mixed herbs
freshly ground pepper and salt

This can be cooked in a large pan on top of the oven
or in a casserole in the oven.

Chop vegetables. Put all ingredients except mushrooms, pepper and olives into a pan or casserole. Cook
on top of oven or in preheated oven, Gas Mark 6
(200C/400F), for 40 minutes. Add other vegetables and
seasoning and cook for a further 10 minutes. Serve with
Lyonnaise potatoes and petits pois.

DAY 8 – POTATO AND HERRING SALAD

2 large potatoes
4 herring fillets
4 medium gherkins

10 ml (2 tsp) reduced calorie mayonnaise
freshly ground black pepper

Boil the potatoes. When cool, cut into small pieces and coat with the mayonnaise. Cut the herring fillets and gherkins into small pieces and mix with the potatoes. Add some freshly ground black pepper.

MUSHROOMS A LA GRECQUE

300 g (12 oz) mushrooms, chopped
1 medium onion, chopped
1 clove garlic, chopped
2 medium tomatoes, chopped
  or 1 small tin tomatoes
1 green pepper, chopped
4 green olives, chopped
5 ml (1 tsp) chopped fresh parsley
  or 3 ml (½ tsp) dried mixed herbs
1 bay leaf
75 ml (3 fl oz) water (unless using tinned tomatoes)
freshly ground pepper and salt

Cook the onion, garlic and tomatoes in the water for 10 minutes. Add all other ingredients except the olives and cook for a further 5 minutes. Garnish with the chopped green olives and serve with brown rice and a green salad.

DAY 9 – BEETROOT AND CHICORY SALAD

4 large cooked beetroot
2 heads chicory
lemon juice
freshly ground black pepper

Cut the beetroot into small pieces or grate it. Cut the

chicory into rings. Put the beetroot onto a plate and surround with the chicory. Dribble over some lemon juice and grind some black pepper onto the salad.

PENNE WITH HAM

100 g (4 oz) penne (or other pasta shapes)
100 g (4 oz) cooked ham, cut into strips
100 g (4 oz) petits pois
1 medium onion, chopped
1 clove garlic, chopped
2 medium courgettes, cut into small pieces
75 g (3 oz) mushrooms, chopped
5 ml (1 tsp) chopped fresh thyme
  or 3 ml (½ tsp) dried mixed herbs
dash Tabasco or chilli sauce
1 small tin tomatoes
freshly ground pepper and salt

Cook the pasta as directed. Cook all other ingredients, except the ham, in the tomatoes, with a little added water if necessary, for 10 minutes. Add the ham for a few moments, then stir the pasta into the sauce. Serve with grated Parmesan cheese and a green salad.

DAY 10 – SWEETCORN AND RED PEPPER MAYONNAISE

1 large tin sweetcorn
1 medium red pepper
1 small onion
10 ml (2 tsp) reduced calorie mayonnaise
cayenne pepper

Cut the red pepper into small pieces and grate the onion. Mix all ingredients together. Dust the top of the salad with cayenne pepper.

MACKEREL IN ORANGE DRESSING

2 mackerel, gutted
juice of 2 oranges
½″ piece root ginger, peeled and shredded
freshly ground black pepper

Place each mackerel in a parcel of foil with the orange juice, ginger and black pepper. Bake in a preheated oven, Gas Mark 6 (200C/400F), for 20 minutes. Serve with brown rice and a chicory and orange salad.

DAY 11 – WALDORF PITTA / OPEN SANDWICH

2 sticks celery
1 red apple
1 green apple
10 ml (2 tsp) chopped walnuts
1 small onion
15 ml (1 tbsp) low fat natural yogurt
lemon juice
freshly ground black pepper

Cut the celery and apples into small pieces and grate the onion. Mix together all ingredients and pile into a wholemeal pitta or onto a slice of wholemeal bread.

LEEKS MORNAY

440 g (1 lb) leeks
1 medium onion, chopped
2 eggs, hard-boiled
150 g (6 oz) low fat Cheddar cheese
300 ml (10 fl oz) skimmed milk
15 g (½ oz) cornflour, mixed with a little water
freshly ground pepper and salt

Cook the leeks and onion in a steamer for 10 minutes. Arrange in an ovenproof dish and put slices of hard-boiled egg on top. Add salt and pepper. Make a white sauce with the milk and cornflour and add most of the grated cheese. Pour the sauce over the leeks and egg. Scatter the remaining grated cheese over the top. Bake in a pre-heated oven, Gas Mark 5 (190C/375F) for 15 minutes. Brown under the grill. Serve with jacket potatoes and a green salad.

DAY 12 – PASTA SALAD

50 g (2 oz) cooked pasta shapes
2 medium tomatoes, cut into small pieces
cucumber, cut into small pieces
8 capers
5 ml (1 tsp) reduced calorie mayonnaise
10 ml (2 tsp) low fat natural yogurt
dash of soy sauce
freshly ground black pepper
lemon wedges

Combine all ingredients. Arrange on a plate and garnish with lemon wedges.

CHINESE PORK FILLET, PRAWNS AND CELERY

100 g (4 oz) pork fillet
100 g (4 oz) prawns
2 sticks of celery
1 medium onion
1 clove garlic
100 g (4 oz) mushrooms
5 ml (1 tsp) soy sauce
5 ml (1 tsp) Teriyaki sauce
150 ml (5 fl oz) water, or wine and water, mixed

5 ml (1 tsp) lemon juice
freshly ground pepper and salt
handful of cashews to garnish

Bake the pork fillet with the lemon juice in foil for 25 minutes in a preheated oven, Gas Mark 6 (200C/400F). When cooked, shred the meat, reserving any juices. Meanwhile, in a wok or a large pan, gently poach the chopped celery, onion and garlic in the wine/water for 5 minutes. Add the chopped mushrooms and cook for a further 5 minutes. Stir in the soy sauce and the Teri-yaki sauce, then add the pork, with any remaining juices, and the prawns. Add salt and pepper. Garnish with cashews. Serve with egg noodles or brown rice.

DAY 13 – JACKET POTATO WITH COTTAGE CHEESE AND KIWI FRUIT

2 large baking potatoes
220 g (8 oz) low fat cottage cheese
2 kiwi fruit

Bake the potatoes, then open them lengthways. Pile the cottage cheese onto the potatoes and arrange slices of kiwi fruit on top.

GIGOT OF MONKFISH

1 medium monkfish tail
300 ml (10 fl oz) cider
5 ml (1 tsp) soy sauce
5 ml (1 tsp) chopped fresh dill
2 sprigs of dill
75 ml (3 fl oz) reduced fat single cream
freshly ground pepper and salt

Put the monkfish into an ovenproof dish. Pour over the cider and soy sauce and add salt and pepper. Cover with foil. Bake in a preheated oven, Gas Mark 5 (190C/375F), for 25 minutes. Remove foil and bake for a further 5 minutes. Pour juices into a pan. Keep the monkfish warm. Reduce cooking liquid to 75 ml (3 fl oz). Stir in the chopped dill and the fresh cream. Cut the sides of the monkfish from the bone and arrange on individual plates. Spoon the sauce onto the plates. Garnish with sprigs of dill. Serve with brown rice or jacket potato and cauliflower florets.

DAY 14 – FENNEL AND SMOKED TROUT SALAD

½ fennel bulb
1 smoked trout fillet
lollo rosso or other salad leaf
2 lime wedges
10 ml (2 tsp) reduced calorie mayonnaise
freshly ground black pepper

Chop the fennel into small pieces and flake the smoked trout. Mix together with the mayonnaise. Serve on individual plates, garnished with lollo rosso and a wedge of lime. Grind some black pepper over the salad.

CHICKEN LOMBATTINI

2 chicken breast fillets
50 g (2 oz) mushrooms
5 ml (1 tsp) lemon juice
dash Tabasco or chilli sauce
½ glass white wine
5 ml (1 tsp) chopped fresh basil
    or 3 ml (½ tsp) dried mixed herbs
10 ml (2 tsp) olive oil
freshly ground pepper and salt
2 wedges of lemon

Cook the chicken gently in olive oil for 8 minutes. Add mushrooms. Pour over wine, lemon juice and chilli sauce. Add herbs, salt and pepper. Garnish with wedges of lemon. Serve with new potatoes and French beans.

DAY 15 – LENTIL AND TOMATO SALAD

75 g (3 oz) lentils, soaked and cooked as directed
2 medium tomatoes, sliced
1 small onion, grated or cut into small pieces
3 ml (½ tsp) mustard
lemon juice
freshly ground black pepper

Mix together the lentils, onion and mustard. Put on a plate and arrange the tomato on top. Squeeze some lemon juice and grind some black pepper onto the salad.

TAGLIATELLE WITH PRAWNS

100 g (4 oz) tagliatelle
150 g (6 oz) cooked prawns
1 medium onion, chopped
1 clove garlic, chopped
75 g (3 oz) mushrooms, chopped
100 g (4 oz) sweetcorn
5 ml (1 tsp) chopped fresh dill
   or 3 ml (½ tsp) dried mixed herbs
5 ml (1 tsp) Nam Pla fish sauce
150 ml (5 fl oz) low-fat single cream
freshly ground pepper and salt

Cook the pasta as directed. Cook the onion and garlic in a little water for 10 minutes. Add the mushrooms, sweetcorn and dill and cook for a further 5 minutes. Reduce liquid if necessary. Pour the cream into the pan and add the prawns, fish sauce, pepper and salt. When the cream and prawns are heated through, arrange the tagliatelle on a serving dish and pour over the sauce. Serve with a green pepper and cucumber salad.

DAY 16 – COURGETTES AND MUSHROOMS WITH RICE

2 medium courgettes, sliced
100 g (4 oz) mushrooms, chopped
1 small onion, chopped
75 g (3 oz) brown rice, cooked
5 ml (1 tsp) chopped fresh parsley
  or 3 ml (½ tsp) dried mixed herbs
soy sauce
lemon juice
freshly ground black pepper and salt
black olives

Gently simmer the courgettes, mushrooms, onion and herbs in water for 10 minutes. Reduce the liquid. Mix vegetables with the rice, soy sauce, lemon juice and pepper and salt. Garnish with black olives.

MAGYAR GOULASH

150 g (6 oz) pork fillet, cut into bite-sized pieces
1 large onion
1 clove garlic
1 large carrot
1 small swede
1 large parsnip
100 g (4 oz) petits pois
100 g (4 oz) cooked Borlotti beans
1 bouquet garni
  or 3 ml (½ tsp) dried mixed herbs
1 bay leaf
10 ml (2 tsp) tomato purée
150 ml (5 fl oz) red wine

150 ml (5 fl oz) boiling water
15 ml (1 tbsp) paprika
freshly ground pepper and salt
soured cream

Clean all vegetables and cut into pieces. Put in a large
casserole with the pork, petits pois, beans and herbs.
Mix together the tomato puree, wine, water, paprika,
pepper and salt and pour over the casserole. Cook in a
preheated oven, Gas Mark 5 (190C/375F), for 1 hour
30 minutes. Garnish with a little soured cream and serve
with Brussels sprouts and jacket potatoes.

DAY 17 – SALMON AND APPLE MAYONNAISE

125 g (5 oz) salmon, cooked and flaked
1 apple, grated or cut into small pieces
15 ml (1 tbsp) pumpkin seeds
5 ml (1 tsp) reduced calorie mayonnaise
10 ml (2 tsp) low fat natural yogurt
freshly ground black pepper
lime wedges

Combine all the ingredients. Arrange on a plate and
garnish with the lime wedges.

MUSHROOM RISOTTO

325 g (12 oz) mushrooms, chopped (use different types
    if possible – oyster, shiitake, cup, brown)
1 medium onion, chopped
1 clove garlic, chopped
100 g (4 oz) petits pois
100 g (4 oz) cooked chick peas
360 ml (12 fl oz) vegetable stock
150 ml (5 fl oz) white wine
150 ml (5 fl oz) water
5 ml (1 tsp) chopped fresh thyme
    or 3 ml (½ tsp) dried mixed herbs

100 g (4 oz) risotto rice
5 ml (1 tsp) sunflower oil
freshly ground pepper and salt
2 wedges of lemon

Gently cook the mushrooms, petits pois, onion and garlic in the vegetable stock and herbs for 5 minutes. Remove the vegetables. Add the wine and water to the cooking liquid. In another pan, warm the sunflower oil. Add the risotto rice and, stirring continuously, cook for 2–3 minutes. Add 150 ml (5 fl oz) of the cooking liquid to the rice and simmer, stirring occasionally, until the liquid is absorbed. Add a further 150 ml (5 fl oz) of the liquid, repeating the process. Finally, add the rest of the liquid and the pepper and salt. If the rice is still not cooked, add some more water. Stir in all the vegetables and garnish the risotto with the lemon wedges.

DAY 18 – TABBOULEH

75 g (3 oz) burghul (cracked wheat)
1 large tomato, cut into very small pieces
piece of cucumber, cut into very small pieces
1 small onion, grated
15 ml (1 tbsp) chopped fresh mint
    or 8 ml (1½ tsp) mint sauce
juice of 1 large lemon
5 ml (1 tsp) olive oil
freshly ground black pepper and salt
lemon wedges

Soak the burghul in lots of cold water for 15 minutes, then rinse and drain, squeezing the water out. Put in a bowl with the lemon juice and the pepper and salt. Leave for a few minutes. Add the olive oil, mint and salad ingredients and mix thoroughly. Garnish with the lemon wedges.

SARDINES PROVENCALES

6 fresh or frozen sardines
1 small tin tomatoes
1 onion, finely chopped
5 ml (1 tsp) chopped fresh parsley
    or 3 ml (½ tsp) dried mixed herbs
1 clove garlic, chopped
5 ml (1 tsp) lemon juice
2 wedges of lemon
freshly ground pepper and salt

Clean, scale and gut the sardines and remove the heads.
Place in an ovenproof serving dish. Add all other
ingredients except wedges of lemon. Cover with foil and
bake for 20 minutes at Gas Mark 6 (200C/400F).
Remove the foil and bake for a further 5 minutes.
Garnish with wedges of lemon. Serve with new potatoes
and a green salad.

DAY 19 – CHICORY, ORANGE AND CUCUMBER PITTA / OPEN SANDWICH

1 head chicory, cut into rings
1 orange, peeled and sliced
piece of cucumber, sliced
10 ml (2 tsp) low fat natural yogurt
orange juice
freshly ground black pepper

Combine salad ingredients with the yogurt and pepper.
Squeeze some fresh orange juice over the salad.

JAMBALAYA

2 turkey breast fillets, cut into small pieces
10 ml (2 tsp) lemon juice
1 medium onion

220g (8 oz) tomatoes, skinned and chopped
  or 1 small tin tomatoes
1 small tin butter beans, drained
2 sticks celery
5 ml (1 tsp) chopped fresh basil
5 ml (1 tsp) chopped fresh parsley
1 bay leaf
2 chopped spring onions
100 g (4 oz) brown rice
chilli sauce
salt and cayenne pepper
2 wedges of lime

Put the turkey with the lemon juice into an ovenproof dish. Cover with foil and bake for 30 minutes in a preheated oven, Gas Mark 6 (200C/400F). Cook the rice. In another pan, cook the chopped onion and celery with the tomatoes and 150 ml (6 fl oz) water, or if using tinned tomatoes omit the water. Add the basil, parsley and bay leaf, salt and cayenne pepper. Stir the rice into the tomato mixture, adding the chilli sauce. Add the beans, pour over the turkey, mix well and continue to cook, covered, in the oven for another 20 minutes. Serve garnished with chopped spring onions and wedges of lime.

DAY 20 – JACKET POTATO WITH HERRING

2 large baking potatoes
4 herring fillets
1 large tomato, cut into small pieces
1 small onion, cut into small pieces
lemon juice
freshly ground black pepper

Bake the potatoes. Mix together the tomato, onion and lemon juice. Arrange all the ingredients on a plate and dust with black pepper.

MEDITERRANEAN VEGETABLES

1 courgette
1 green pepper
1 beef tomato
1 small onion
1 clove garlic
100 g (4 oz) cooked chick peas
½ cup cooked brown rice
5 ml (1 tsp) soy sauce
5 ml (1 tsp) tomato purée
75 ml (3 fl oz) white wine
75 ml (3 fl oz) water
10 ml (2 tsp) chopped fresh basil
   or 5 ml (1 tsp) dried mixed herbs
freshly ground pepper and salt
lightly toasted pine nuts or flaked almonds

Cut the courgette in half lengthways and scoop out
inner flesh. Cut the pepper in half lengthways and
remove seeds and stem. Cut the tomato in half and
scoop out flesh. Cook the chopped onion, garlic, courgette flesh and tomato flesh in the wine and water mixed
with the soy sauce and tomato purée. When cooked,
drain and reserve the liquid. Add the rice, cooked chick
peas, herbs, salt and pepper to the onion mixture.
Arrange in the vegetable shells. Put them in an ovenproof dish and pour over the cooking liquid. Cover
with foil and bake for 30 minutes in a preheated oven,
Gas Mark 6 (200C/400F). Garnish with the nuts. Serve
with a green salad.

DAY 21 – SOYA BEAN CASSEROLE

150 g (6 oz) soya beans, soaked and cooked as directed
1 large onion
1 clove garlic

1 large carrot
2 sticks celery
1 large tin tomatoes
10 ml (2 tsp) tomato purée
5 ml (1 tsp) chopped fresh parsley
   or 3 ml (½ tsp) dried mixed herbs
1 bay leaf
5 ml (1 tsp) paprika
soy sauce
freshly ground black pepper and salt

Chop the onion, garlic, carrot and celery and put into a casserole with the soya beans. Add all the other ingredients, cover the casserole and cook in a preheated oven, Gas Mark 6 (200C/400F), for 1 hour 30 minutes.

VENISON WITH BLACK CHERRIES

2 x 125 g (5 oz) venison steaks
220 g (8 oz) tinned black cherries, pitted
150 ml (5 fl oz) juice of black cherries
1 glass red wine

Grill the venison steaks. Heat the black cherries with the juice and red wine. Reduce the liquid. Put the meat onto a plate and pour the sauce and cherries around it. Serve with parsnip purée and red cabbage.

DAY 22 – FETA AND BACON SALAD

3 large raw spinach leaves, washed
1 small onion
1 small green pepper
3 slices bacon, cut into strips
50 g (2 oz) Feta cheese
100 g (4 oz) cooked Borlotti beans
10 ml (2 tsp) lemon juice
5 ml (1 tsp) olive oil

freshly ground black pepper
wedges of lemon

Cut spinach into pieces. Finely chop onion (and if possible soak in cold water for 30 minutes). Cut pepper into pieces and the Feta cheese into cubes. Arrange all these with the Borlotti beans on individual plates. Gently cook the bacon strips in the olive oil. At the last moment, add the lemon juice and black pepper to the bacon. Arrange pieces of bacon on each plate and pour over the warm dressing. Garnish with wedges of lemon.

FENNEL PROVENCAL

2 fennel bulbs
220 g (8 oz) tomatoes, chopped
   or 1 large tin chopped tomatoes
1 medium onion, chopped
1 clove garlic, chopped
100 g (4 oz) mushrooms, chopped
1 red pepper, chopped
5 ml (1 tsp) chopped fresh parsley
   or 3 ml (½ tsp) dried mixed herbs
freshly ground pepper and salt

Cook the tomatoes in 225 ml (8 fl oz) of water, unless using tinned tomatoes. Trim the fennel, cut into quarters and core. Cook all ingredients, except the mushrooms and pepper, in a saucepan for 30 minutes. Add the mushrooms and pepper and cook for a further 10 minutes. Serve with brown rice and a cucumber and black olive salad.

DAY 23 – MANGETOUT, TOMATO AND CASHEW NUT SALAD

100 g (4 oz) mangetout, lightly cooked
2 medium tomatoes, sliced
15 ml (1 tbsp) cashew nuts, chopped

lemon juice
cayenne pepper

Arrange the mangetout and tomato on a plate. Squeeze over some lemon juice. Garnish with the chopped cashew nuts and dust the salad with a little cayenne pepper.

SAUMON AUX EPINARDS

2 x 125 g (5 oz) fillets of salmon, skinned
10/12 large spinach leaves
2 lime wedges

Blanch the spinach leaves in boiling water for about 30 seconds, then dry with a paper towel. Wrap 5/6 leaves around each salmon fillet. Steam in a vegetable steamer over boiling water for 5 minutes. Garnish with lime wedges and serve with new potatoes and French beans.

DAY 24 – BROAD BEAN AND HAM MAYONNAISE

150 g (6 oz) broad beans, lightly cooked
75 g (3 oz) lean cooked ham, shredded
1 small red pepper, cut into small pieces
5 ml (1 tsp) reduced calorie mayonnaise
10 ml (2 tsp) low fat natural yogurt
lemon juice
freshly ground black pepper

Combine the broad beans and ham with the mayonnaise, yogurt and lemon juice. Scatter pieces of red pepper over the salad and grind some black pepper on the top.

LAMB KOFTAS

220 g (8 oz) minced lamb
1 small onion, grated
5 ml (1 tsp) ground coriander
5 ml (1 tsp) chopped fresh parsley
freshly ground pepper and salt

Soak 4 6" kebab sticks in water to prevent burning when cooking. Mix all the ingredients together and separate into 8 balls. Flatten into a sausage shape and put 2 pieces of meat onto each kebab. Cook under a moderately hot grill for about 10 minutes. Garnish with a wedge of lemon. Serve with brown rice and a green salad.

DAY 25 – SPINACH, COTTAGE CHEESE AND PEAR SALAD

raw spinach leaves, shredded
100 g (4 oz) low fat cottage cheese
2 pears, cut into small pieces
lemon juice
freshly ground black pepper

Arrange the shredded spinach leaves on a plate. Mix together the cottage cheese and pear and pile on top. Squeeze some lemon juice over the salad and add a little black pepper.

TUNA TORTIGLIONI

100 g (4 oz) tortiglioni
150 g (6 oz) fresh tuna, grilled for 4 minutes, then flaked
    or 200 g (8 oz) tin tuna in brine, drained
1 medium onion, chopped
1 clove garlic, chopped
75 g (3 oz) mushrooms, chopped
2 sticks celery, chopped

1 small tin tomatoes
1 bouquet garni
   or 3 ml (½ tsp) dried mixed herbs
1 glass white wine and water mixed
freshly ground pepper and salt

Cook the tortiglioni as directed. Cook the onion, garlic, mushrooms and celery in the tomatoes and wine/water with the bouquet garni. Add the flaked tuna and salt and pepper, then mix with the tortiglioni. Serve with a red kidney bean salad.

DAY 26 – CRAB AND WATERCRESS PITTA / OPEN SANDWICH

1 medium dressed crab
watercress
lime juice
cayenne pepper

Mix all ingredients together and pile into wholemeal pitta or onto a slice of wholemeal bread.

AUBERGINE AND COURGETTE KEBABS

1 small courgette
1 small aubergine
1 small onion
1 medium tomato
4 mushrooms
1 small green pepper
100 ml (4 fl oz) white wine
15 ml (1 tbsp) lemon juice
1 clove garlic, chopped
3 ml (½ tsp) dried mixed herbs
freshly ground pepper and salt

Soak 4 6″ kebab sticks in water for 30 minutes to prevent burning when cooking the kebabs. Cut all the vegetables to make up 4 kebabs. Mix all the other ingredients to make a marinade and put the kebabs into the marinade for about 40 minutes. Grill the kebabs, turning frequently. Serve with a jacket potato and a green salad.

DAY 27 – JACKET POTATO WITH TUNA MAYONNAISE

2 large baking potatoes
200 g (8 oz) tin tuna in brine, drained and flaked
2 medium gherkins, chopped
10 ml (2 tsp) reduced calorie mayonnaise

Bake the potatoes and open them lengthways. Mix together the other ingredients and pile onto the potatoes.

CHICKEN AND SEAFOOD PAELLA

2 small chicken breast fillets
50 g (2 oz) cooked prawns
2 squid, prepared
50 g (2 oz) cooked mussels
100 g (4 oz) rice
1 medium onion
100 g (4oz) frozen petits pois
50 g (2 oz) mushrooms
1 green or red pepper
1 clove garlic
10 ml (2 tsp) chopped fresh parsley
    or 5 ml (1 tsp) dried mixed herbs
5 ml (1 tsp) Nam Pla fish sauce
5 ml (1 tsp) lemon juice
freshly ground pepper and salt
few strands saffron
    or 3 ml (½ tsp) turmeric powder
wedges of lemon

large prawns and mussels – optional – to garnish

A wok is ideal for making paella; otherwise use a large frying pan.

Cook rice with the saffron or turmeric in a medium pan. Chop onion and chicken into small pieces and cook with petits pois in water or, if desired, white wine with water, in the wok or frying pan for 10 minutes. Cut squid into rings and cook with chicken for 5 minutes. Add chopped mushrooms, pepper, garlic and herbs. Add rice to the pan and also fish sauce, lemon juice and salt and pepper to taste. Immediately prior to serving, add the prawns and mussels and amalgamate all ingredients, taking care not to break up the fish. Garnish with wedges of lemon and, if desired, large prawns and mussels.

DAY 28 – MARINATED HERRINGS

---

4 herring fillets
4 gherkins, finely chopped
1 small onion, finely chopped
1 medium onion, coarsely chopped
1 bay leaf
4 cloves
pinch of salt
8 black peppercorns
5 ml (1 tsp) brown sugar
75 ml (3 fl oz) white wine vinegar
75 ml (3 fl oz) water

Lay the herring fillets skin side down and put some of the finely chopped onion and gherkin mixture on each. Roll the fillets up and secure with a cocktail stick. Put them in a heatproof dish. Meanwhile, put all the other ingredients into a pan, bring to the boil and simmer for about 5 minutes to let the flavours mingle. Pour over the herring rolls. When cool, cover and put in the

refrigerator for at least 3 days. To serve, remove the
cocktail sticks and unroll. Serve with wedges of wholemeal bread.

MEXICAN BEEF

150 g (6 oz) fillet or sirloin steak
1 medium onion
1 clove garlic
1 green pepper
1 red pepper
100 g (4 oz) mushrooms
1 small tin red kidney beans, drained
½ green chilli, de-seeded
5 ml (1 tsp) tomato purée
150 ml (5 fl oz) water, or wine and water, mixed
chilli sauce
10 ml (2 tsp) sunflower oil
freshly ground pepper and salt

Poach the chopped onion and garlic in the 150 ml wine/
water for 5 minutes. Add the chopped, de-seeded peppers and chilli and the sliced mushrooms, then cook for
a further 5 minutes. Remove the vegetables and keep
warm. Reduce the juices and stir in the tomato purée,
chilli sauce and salt and pepper. Return the vegetables
to the pan and keep warm, then add the red kidney
beans. Meanwhile, cut the steak into slivers, ½″ wide
by 1″, as thinly as possible – this is more easily done if
the meat is put into the freezer about 30 minutes before
being cut. Gently cook in hot sunflower oil for 3–4
minutes. Stir the meat into the vegetables and serve
immediately with brown rice or jacket potatoes and a
green salad.

DAY 29 – PASTA AND PEPPER SALAD

50 g (2 oz) pasta shapes, cooked
1 small red pepper, cut into small pieces
1 small green pepper, cut into small pieces
small bunch of grapes, halved and seeded
5 ml (1 tsp) reduced calorie mayonnaise
10 ml (2 tsp) low fat natural yogurt

Mix together the pasta shapes, peppers, mayonnaise and yogurt.
Garnish with the grapes.

SWEETCORN MORNAY

2 corn cobs, corn sliced off
  or 1 large tin sweetcorn, drained
2 eggs, hard-boiled and cut into pieces
125 g (5 oz) low fat natural yogurt
125 g (5 oz) low fat Cheddar cheese, grated
freshly ground black pepper

Mix together the corn, egg and yogurt and put into an ovenproof dish. Scatter the grated cheese over the top and grind some black pepper onto the dish. Bake in a preheated oven, Gas Mark 5 (190C/375F), for 15 minutes. Brown under the grill. Serve with new potatoes and a tomato and onion salad.

DAY 30 – PRAWN AND RICE SHELLS

100 g (4 oz) cooked prawns
50 g (2 oz) brown rice
25 g (1 oz) frozen petits pois
12 pistachio nuts, shelled
3 ml (½ tsp) soy sauce
5 ml (1 tsp) lemon juice
5 ml (1 tsp) reduced calorie mayonnaise

freshly ground pepper and salt
2 sprigs of parsley

Cook the rice as indicated on the packet and cook the
frozen petits pois with the rice for the last few minutes.
Cut the prawns and the nuts into small pieces and, when
the rice and petits pois are cold, mix together. Gently
stir in the other ingredients and arrange in scallop shells
or on a plate. Chill before serving. Garnish with sprigs
of parsley.

CHICKEN IN MINT AND YOGURT MARINADE

---

2 chicken breast fillets
125 g (5 oz) low-fat natural yogurt
5 ml (1 tsp) chopped fresh mint
    or 3 ml (½ tsp) mint sauce
freshly ground black pepper
2 lemon wedges

Remove any skin or bone from the chicken. Cut two
slits into the top of each piece of chicken. Mix together
the yogurt, mint and black pepper. Put the chicken into
the marinade and leave for at least 1 hour. Grill the
chicken for 10 minutes on each side. Garnish with lemon
wedges and serve with a jacket potato and broad beans.

BREAKFAST

After approximately ten hours of fasting, the body
needs a good source of energy for the rigours of
the day to come. Many people make do with a cup
of coffee which, although it may taste good, does
little to support you until lunchtime. And it may
tempt you into a mid-morning snack of chocolate
biscuits or worse.

People who skip breakfast work less

efficiently than people who have taken the trouble to provide themselves with fuel for the morning. Other people, however, have a long tradition of breakfasting wholeheartedly, but perhaps in a way that is not wholesome for the heart.

Cereals are an excellent source of energy and there are a large number of packet cereals available. As a change and to provide more nourishment, try pouring yogurt over them and topping them with fresh fruit. Porridge can be made up as directed. Stir a little honey in to sweeten when ready to eat. Try making your own muesli rather than buying well-known brands.

Eggs are a good source of protein but they should be cooked without using fat. Poach, boil or scramble the eggs, or make into an omelette in a non-stick pan with a minimum of low-fat margarine. Chop a little cooked ham, tomato or mushroom into a scrambled egg or an omelette as a variation. Add small pieces of smoked salmon for a delicious breakfast!

Fish is an excellent food: try kedgeree as an enjoyable breakfast dish. Home-cooked ham, accompanied by fresh brown bread, is also a nourishing start to the day.

A very low-fat start to the day is tomatoes or mushrooms on a slice of wholemeal toast; and the baked bean must not be forgotten at this time of day. A small tin of baked beans on a slice of wholemeal toast will provide you with 19 grams of fibre, and help get you through the morning. (Add a teaspoonful of curry powder, or mix in some red kidney beans and a little chilli sauce for variations on the baked bean theme.)

Eating fruit is a very refreshing start to the day. Prunes should not be underestimated (4 ounces contain 8 grams of fibre). They provide one of the top sources of carbohydrate. Prunes can be added to other dried fruit to make a fruit compote, or to a muesli; add pumpkin, sunflower or sesame seeds to provide further vital nutrients.

Chop and mix together two or three pieces of fresh fruit. Squeeze a little fresh orange juice over the fruit – you can almost taste the energy!

Freshly juiced vegetables or fruit provide an excellent meal-in-a-glass. Carrot juice contains many vitamins, including vitamin A, and is the ideal mixer for other vegetable juices. It can easily be mixed with orange or apple juice, if preferred. Experiment with different juices and combinations.

With a little time and imagination, there is no end to the low fat, high fibre energy breakfasts you can make for yourself.

KEDGEREE

75 g (3 oz) rice
150 g (6 oz) smoked haddock
1 medium onion, chopped
1 egg, hard-boiled and chopped
5 ml (1 tsp) garam masala, optional
3 ml (½ tsp) chopped fresh parsley
freshly ground pepper and salt

Poach the smoked haddock with the onion in water. Skin, then flake the fish and keep warm. Cook the rice with the garam masala, using cooking liquid and extra water as required. When the rice is cooked, gently mix in all other ingredients. Serve with triangles of toast.

YORK HAM WITH MELON AND KIWI FRUIT

2 slices York ham
¼ Cantaloup melon

1 kiwi fruit
freshly ground black pepper

Arrange the ham with slices of the skinned fruit on top.
Grind a little black pepper over the fruit. Serve with a
wholemeal roll.

FRUIT COMPOTE

50 g (2 oz) dried apricots
75 g (3 oz) dried pears
75 g (3 oz) dried prunes
cinnamon powder

Soak the fruit overnight. Mix together thoroughly. Dust
the top of the fruit with some cinnamon powder.

MUESLI

30 ml (2 tbsp) oats
10 ml (2 tsp) bran
5 ml (1 tsp) split almonds
5 ml (1 tsp) pumpkin seeds
5 ml (1 tsp) sesame seeds
1 apple, cut into small pieces or grated
10 ml (2 tsp) raisins
skimmed milk
low fat natural yogurt

Soak the oats and bran in skimmed milk overnight. Add
all other ingredients and mix thoroughly. Top with low-
fat natural yogurt and, if desired, any other fresh fruit
available.

DEVILLED BACON

3 slices lean bacon
2 tomatoes, chopped

cayenne pepper
3 ml (½ tsp) mustard

Grill the bacon, then cut into small pieces. Meanwhile, cook the tomatoes in a little water. Add the cayenne pepper and mustard. Reduce the liquid if necessary, then add the bacon. Serve with triangles of wholemeal toast.

EATING OUT AND ENTERTAINING

Eating out should not pose a problem even when following the Walking Diet. Avoid all fatty foods and dishes with rich sauces. Choose grilled fish or meat and ask for the accompanying vegetables to be served without butter, or have a salad, dressed simply with lemon juice rather than with French dressing. For dessert, select some fresh fruit. Most restaurants will be able to offer you such foods.

If you are entertaining at home, use the main meal recipe from the Walking Diet for that day or choose another main meal recipe if you so wish. Some of the light meal dishes could be used as a first course, such as Salade Niçoise or Feta and Bacon Salad, but here are some recipes for first courses and some for desserts.

CHICKEN LAO-TSE

2 small chicken breast fillets
Soy sauce
small piece root ginger, peeled and finely chopped
5 ml (1 tsp) clear honey
Iceberg lettuce leaves
piece of cucumber, cut into thin shreds
4 spring onions, cut into thin shreds
plum sauce (available from Oriental delicatessens)

Combine the soy sauce, ginger and honey and marinade

the chicken in it for at least one hour. Grill the chicken for 10 minutes on each side, then shred the meat. Serve the shredded chicken and the other ingredients in individual dishes. Each person should make up Iceberg lettuce 'pancakes'.

SEAFOOD SALAD

2 squid, cleaned and cut into rings
50 g (2 oz) cooked mussels
100 g (4 oz) cooked prawns
50 g (2 oz) cooked clams
5 ml (1 tsp) chopped fresh parsley
   or 3 ml (½ tsp) dried mixed herbs
1 clove garlic, finely chopped
lemon juice
lemon wedges
freshly ground black pepper

Simmer the squid rings in water for 8 minutes, then cool. Combine all ingredients. Arrange in scallop shells or on a plate. Garnish with lemon wedges.

DOLMADES

8 vine leaves, soaked in cold water
75 g (3 oz) brown rice, cooked
10 ml (2 tsp) chopped fresh mint
   or 5 ml (1 tsp) mint sauce
lemon juice
freshly ground black pepper
lemon wedges

Combine the rice, mint, lemon juice and black pepper. Put a spoonful of the mixture in the middle of each vine leaf and roll up, securing the edges, into cigar shapes. Put the stuffed vine leaves into a saucepan and cover with water. Simmer for 30 minutes. They may be served hot or cold. Garnish with lemon wedges and serve with a tomato and onion salad.

VENETIAN PRAWNS

150 g (6 oz) cooked prawns
2 medium tomatoes, chopped
1 small onion, cut into small pieces
1 clove garlic, chopped
5 ml (1 tsp) chopped fresh parsley
   or 3 ml (½ tsp) dried mixed herbs
150 ml (5 fl oz) white wine and water mixed
5 ml (1 tsp) Nam Pla fish sauce
freshly ground black pepper

Gently cook the tomatoes, onion and garlic in the white wine and water. Add the fish sauce, herbs and black pepper. Reduce the liquid if necessary. Add the prawns until heated through. Serve with triangles of wholemeal toast.

CHESTNUT SOUP

220 g (8 oz) chestnut purée
300 ml (10 fl oz) chicken (or vegetable) stock
15 ml (1 tbsp) sherry
15 ml (1 tbsp) reduced fat single cream
freshly ground black pepper

Put the chestnut purée and the stock into a saucepan. Stir over a low heat until smooth. (Whizz in a food processor if possible.) At the last moment, add the sherry and the cream. Serve in individual soup bowls, with a swirl of cream if desired. Grind some black pepper onto the soup.

CRAB AND DILL OMELETTE

1 small dressed crab
  or 125 g (5 oz) tinned crabmeat
2 eggs
5 ml (1 tsp) chopped fresh dill
2 small fronds of dill for garnish
freshly ground black pepper and salt
radicchio or other salad leaves
2 wedges of lime

Whisk the eggs with a little water, adding pepper and salt and the chopped dill. Stir into this mixture the brown meat from the crab, or half of the tinned crabmeat. Using a non-stick omelette pan, adding a little oil if necessary, cook the omelette. At the last moment, add the rest of the crabmeat and fold the omelette over. Cut in half and put a frond of dill on each half. Serve on individual plates, each garnished with radicchio leaves and a lime wedge.

GAZPACHO

½ kg (1 lb) tomatoes, skinned
  or 1 large tin chopped tomatoes
2 medium courgettes
1 small onion
¼ cucumber
½ green pepper
1 clove garlic
10 ml (2 tsp) chopped fresh basil
  or 5 ml (1 tsp) dried mixed herbs
300 ml (10 fl oz) chicken stock
150 ml (5 fl oz) water or white wine mixed with water
freshly ground pepper and salt

Chop vegetables then blend all ingredients in a food processor or liquidiser. Chill for at least 2 hours. (If short of time, add a few ice cubes.) Serve separate small bowls of chopped cucumber, onion, red and green pepper to be added at the table.

SMOKED FISH HORS D'OEUVRE

2 slices smoked salmon
1 smoked mackerel fillet
1 smoked trout fillet
curly endive or other salad leaf
2 wedges of lime
dash of lime or lemon juice
freshly ground black pepper

Arrange the slice of smoked salmon and half fillet of smoked mackerel and smoked trout on a bed of curly endive or other salad leaf. Dribble a little lime or lemon juice and grind some black pepper over each plate. Garnish with a wedge of lime.

ANTIPASTO AMALFI

4 slices Italian salami (such as Napoli)
2 slices Parma ham
4 artichoke hearts, tinned
8 black olives
2 leaves radicchio or other salad leaf
2 wedges lemon
dash of lemon juice
freshly ground black pepper

Arrange on individual plates. Dribble some lemon juice and grind some black pepper over each plate.

SMOKED SALMON PATE

100 g (4 oz) smoked salmon (end cuts are excellent for this)

100 g (4 oz) low fat cottage cheese
5 ml (1 tsp) lemon juice
freshly ground black pepper
2 wedges of lime or lemon
4 pieces of chicory, cut in rings
   or any other salad leaf
toast triangles

Put smoked salmon, cottage cheese, lemon juice and
some freshly ground black pepper into a food processor
and whizz until smooth. Garnish with salad leaf, a
wedge of lime or lemon and a few grinds of black
pepper. Serve toast triangles separately.

FRUIT KEBABS

8 small strawberries
4 pieces pineapple
1 fig, quartered
1 nectarine, cut into 8
1 kiwi fruit, quartered
4 mint leaves
lemon juice

Using 6″ kebab sticks, prepare 4 kebabs with a mint leaf
in the middle. Dribble a little lemon juice over each
kebab. Serve on a platter lined with vine leaves.

EXOTIC FRUIT SALAD

½ mango
1 carambola (star fruit)
¼ pineapple
1 kiwi fruit
1 banana
small bunch each white and black grapes
½ tin lychees in natural juice

Cut the carambola into ⅓″ slices and cut off skin, leaving the star shape intact. Cut all other fruit into bite-size pieces. Mix together the fruit and the juice. Chill for at least 1 hour.

RASPBERRY SORBET

220 g (8 oz) raspberries
juice of ¼ lemon
100 ml (4 fl oz) syrup, made with water and saccharin

Blend the raspberries in a food processor or liquidiser until smooth. Rub the purée through a nylon sieve. Stir in the lemon juice and the syrup. Chill the mixture. If there is a sorbetière available, churn for about 8 minutes, then freeze. If not, after chilling, pour into a freezer tray, cover and freeze for several hours. Blend to break up the ice into finer particles and once more freeze. Take the sorbet out of the freezer 5 or 10 minutes before serving.

PINEAPPLE SICILIANA

1 small pineapple
1 kiwi fruit
1 bunch black grapes
Kirsch (optional)

Cut pineapple into half, lengthways, leaving the leaves on. Cut the flesh loose (a grapefruit knife is useful) and cut into small pieces. Peel and chop kiwi fruit. Halve grapes and remove pips. Mix fruit together and put into pineapple shells. Pour over a little kirsch if desired.

BASKET OF MELON AND GRAPES

1 medium Galia melon
100 g (4 oz) seedless grapes
toasted flaked almonds

Cut off top of melon. Scoop out seeds and discard, then cut out as much flesh as possible, leaving skin intact. Chop flesh and mix with grapes. Put the fruit back into the melon shell and chill. Immediately before serving, decorate with toasted almonds.

MARINATED STRAWBERRIES

1 punnet strawberries
100 ml (4 fl oz) dessert wine

Marinate strawberries for at least 2 hours. They are especially delicious when a small glass of dessert wine is drunk with them.

SPICED BANANAS

2 bananas
lemon juice
brown sugar
cinnamon powder

Cut each banana lengthways and lay on a piece of foil which has been lightly rubbed with low fat margarine to prevent sticking. Squeeze some lemon juice and sprinkle some brown sugar and cinnamon over each banana. Bake the parcels in a preheated oven, Gas Mark 4 (180C/350F), for 25 minutes. Serve in the foil, opening the parcels at the table, so that the full aroma of banana and cinnamon may be enjoyed.

PEARS IN RED WINE

2 pears
125 ml (5 fl oz) red wine
75 ml (3 fl oz) water
10 ml (2 tsp) saccharin

Peel pears, leaving their shape intact. Put into a pan with the wine, water and saccharin. Poach gently for 12 minutes. They may be served warm or chilled.

ORANGES VALENCIANA

4 small juicy oranges
15 ml (1 tbsp) fresh orange juice
30 ml (2 tbsp) orange blossom water
cinnamon powder

Cut the peel from the oranges, leaving the fruits whole. Pour over the orange juice and orange blossom water. Cut fine strips of peel from half of one orange and remove the pith. Simmer the peel strips in two or three changes of water, until soft. Garnish with the peel strips and a dusting of cinnamon.

MELON SALAD

⅛ watermelon
⅛ Piel de Sapo melon
¼ Cantaloup melon
raspberries to garnish

Cut all melons into 2 slices and remove the skin. Arrange on individual plates, garnished with a few raspberries.

SHOPPING LISTS

Life is often so busy that it is difficult always to have the necessary foods that you need in the house. The following lists are to help you stock up for the Walking Diet.

STORE CUPBOARD LIST

tomato purée   chopped tomatoes

red kidney beans

chilli beans

tinned tuna in brine

tinned clams

rice – brown

    white

    risotto

pasta – spaghetti, wholewheat

    tortiglioni

    penne

    tagliatelle

butter beans

baked beans

tinned salmon

dried mixed herbs

bouquet garni

couscous

sweetcorn

olives

anchovies

eggs

Nam Pla fish sauce (available from Oriental food shops)

Tabasco or chilli sauce

lychees

ground coriander

    cumin

    turmeric

    chilli

cinnamon powder

black peppercorns

ground almonds

pine nuts

sunflower seeds

raisins

cereals

black cherries

rhubarb

low calorie sweetener

orange blossom water

olive oil

sunflower oil

Lo-salt

sea salt

split almonds

pumpkin seeds

sesame seeds

sultanas

lentils

FRIDGE LIST

skimmed milk

reduced calorie

  mayonnaise

lemons

natural yogurt

cooked ham

Feta cheese

low fat spread or

    margarine

low fat cottage cheese

limes

marinated herrings

bacon

reduced fat Cheddar

    cheese

FREEZER LIST

(Many of these can be bought fresh, but if this is not possible, keep them in the freezer)

wholemeal bread	wholemeal pitta bread
petits pois	broad beans
fresh salmon	chicken breast fillets
turkey breast fillets	swordfish
mackerel	pork fillet
prawns	monkfish
minced lamb	fresh sardines
venison	fresh tuna
fillet or sirloin steak	raspberries
mangetout	

GREENGROCER LIST

(To be bought as required)

watercress	salad leaves
chicory	onions
courgettes	aubergines
celery	mushrooms
beetroot	spinach
potatoes	sweetcorn
peppers	fennel
tomatoes	garlic
apples	oranges
pears	strawberries
raspberries	grapes
lemons	limes
rhubarb	mango
melon – Galia	carambola (star fruit)
Cantaloup	pineapple
Piel de Sapo	kiwi fruit
watermelon	bananas
figs	nectarines
herbs – parsley	
mint	
dill	
basil	

CHAPTER 5

FAT & FIBRE COUNTER

This chapter is for reference purposes. It consists of the fat and fibre content (per 100 g) of the foods to be found in the Walking Diet and of many other foods, for reasons of comparison. The following symbols should be noted:

Tr Trace
() Estimated value
– No information available

VEGETABLES	Fat g	Fibre g
Artichokes – globe, boiled	Tr	–
Artichokes – Jerusalem, boiled	Tr	–
Asparagus – boiled	Tr	1.5
Aubergine – raw	Tr	2.5
Beans – French, boiled	Tr	3.2
runner, boiled	0.2	3.4
broad, boiled	0.6	4.2
butter, boiled	0.3	5.1
haricot, boiled	0.5	7.4
baked, canned in tomato sauce	0.5	7.3
red kidney, raw	1.7	(25.0)
soya, raw	17.7	–
Beetroot – raw	Tr	3.1
boiled	Tr	2.5
Broccoli tops – raw	Tr	3.6
boiled	Tr	4.1

	Fat g	Fibre g
Brussels sprouts – raw	Tr	4.2
boiled	Tr	2.9
Cabbage – red, raw	Tr	3.4
Savoy, raw	Tr	3.1
boiled	Tr	2.5
spring, boiled	Tr	2.2
white, raw	Tr	2.7
winter, raw	Tr	3.4
boiled	Tr	2.8
Carrots – old, raw	Tr	2.9
boiled	Tr	3.1
young, boiled	Tr	3.0
canned	Tr	3.7
Cauliflower – raw	Tr	2.1
boiled	Tr	1.8
Celeriac – boiled	Tr	4.9
Celery – raw	Tr	1.8
boiled	Tr	2.2
Chicory – raw	Tr	–
Courgettes – raw	0.4	–
Cucumber – raw	0.1	0.4
Endive – raw	Tr	2.2
Garlic – raw	0.3	–
Leeks – raw	Tr	3.1
boiled	Tr	3.9
Lentils – split, boiled	0.5	3.7
Lettuce – raw	0.4	1.5
Marrow – raw	Tr	(1.8)
Mushrooms – raw	0.6	2.5
Mustard and cress – raw	Tr	3.7
Okra – raw	Tr	(3.2)
Onions – raw	Tr	1.3
boiled	Tr	1.3
fried	33.3	(4.5)
spring, raw	Tr	3.1
Parsley – raw	Tr	9.1

	Fat g	Fibre g
Parsnips – raw	Tr	4.0
boiled	Tr	2.5
Peas – fresh, raw	0.4	5.2
boiled	0.4	5.2
frozen, raw	0.4	7.8
boiled	0.4	12.0
canned, garden	0.3	6.3
processed	0.4	7.9
dried, boiled	0.4	4.8
split, dried, boiled	0.3	5.1
chick, raw	5.7	(15.0)
Peppers – green, raw	0.4	0.9
boiled	0.4	0.9
Potatoes – old, boiled	0.1	1.0
mashed (with margarine and milk)	5.0	0.9
baked	0.1	2.5
baked (weighed with skins)	0.1	2.0
roast (shallow fat)	4.8	–
chips (deep fat)	10.9	–
chips, frozen	3.0	1.9
frozen, fried	18.9	3.2
new, boiled	0.1	2.0
instant, made up	0.2	3.6
crisps	35.9	11.9
Pumpkin – raw	Tr	0.5
Radishes – raw	Tr	1.0
Spinach – boiled	0.5	6.3
Spring greens – boiled	Tr	3.8
Swedes – boiled	Tr	2.8

	Fat g	Fibre g
Sweetcorn – on-the-cob, raw	2.4	3.7
boiled	2.3	4.7
– canned kernels	(0.5)	5.7
Tomatoes – raw	Tr	1.5
fried	5.9	3.0
canned	Tr	0.9
Turnips – boiled	0.3	2.2
Vine leaves	–	5.0
Watercress – raw	Tr	3.3

FRUIT

	Fat g	Fibre g
Apples – eating, flesh only	Tr	2.0
cooking, raw, flesh only	Tr	2.4
baked without sugar	Tr	2.5
stewed without sugar	Tr	2.1
Apricots – fresh, raw	Tr	2.1
stewed without sugar	Tr	1.7
dried, raw	Tr	24.0
stewed without sugar	Tr	8.9
Avocado pears	22.2	2.0
Bananas – raw	0.3	3.4
Blackberries – raw	Tr	7.3
stewed without sugar	Tr	6.3
Cherries – eating, raw	Tr	1.7
cooking, raw	Tr	1.7
stewed without sugar	Tr	1.4
Cranberries – raw	Tr	4.2
Currants – black, raw	Tr	8.7
stewed without sugar	Tr	7.4
red, raw	Tr	8.2
stewed without sugar	Tr	7.0
Damsons – raw	Tr	4.1
stewed without sugar	Tr	3.5
stewed with sugar	Tr	3.1

	Fat g	Fibre g
Dates – dried	Tr	8.7
Figs – green, raw	Tr	2.5
dried, raw	Tr	18.5
stewed without sugar	Tr	10.3
Gooseberries – green, raw	Tr	3.2
stewed without sugar	Tr	2.7
Grapes – black, raw	Tr	0.4
white, raw	Tr	0.9
Grapefruit – raw	Tr	0.6
canned	Tr	0.4
Greengages – raw	Tr	2.6
stewed without sugar	Tr	2.2
Guavas – canned	Tr	3.6
Lemons – whole	Tr	5.2
juice, fresh	Tr	0
Lychees – raw	Tr	(0.5)
canned	Tr	0.4
Mandarin oranges – canned	Tr	0.3
Mangoes – raw	Tr	(1.5)
Melons – Cantaloup, raw	Tr	1.0
yellow, Honeydew, raw	Tr	0.9
watermelon, raw	Tr	–
Nectarines – raw	Tr	2.4
Olives – in brine	11.0	4.4
Oranges – raw	Tr	2.0
juice, fresh	Tr	0
Passion fruit – raw	Tr	15.9
Paw paw – canned	Tr	0.5
Peaches – fresh, raw	Tr	1.4
Pears – eating	Tr	2.3
cooking, raw	Tr	2.9
stewed without sugar	Tr	2.5
stewed with sugar	Tr	2.3

	Fat g	Fibre g
Pineapple – fresh	Tr	1.2
canned	Tr	0.9
Plums – Victoria dessert, raw	Tr	2.1
cooking, raw	Tr	2.5
stewed without sugar	Tr	2.2
Prunes – dried, raw	Tr	16.1
stewed without sugar	Tr	8.1
Quinces – raw	Tr	6.4
Raisins – dried	Tr	6.8
Raspberries – raw	Tr	7.4
Rhubarb – raw	Tr	2.6
stewed without sugar	Tr	2.4
Strawberries – raw	Tr	2.2
Sultanas – dried	Tr	7.0
Tangerines – raw	Tr	1.9

FISH AND FISH PRODUCTS

White fish

	Fat g	Fibre g
Cod – raw, fresh fillets	0.7	0
fried in batter	10.3	0
poached in milk (butter added)	1.1	0
steamed	0.9	0
smoked, poached	1.6	0
Haddock – raw, fresh	0.6	0
fried	8.3	0
steamed	0.8	0
smoked, steamed	0.9	0
Halibut – raw	2.4	0
Lemon Sole – raw	1.4	0
Plaice – raw	2.2	0

	Fat g	Fibre g
Fatty fish		
Anchovies – canned in oil, fish only	19.9	0
Herring – raw	18.5	0
grilled	13.0	0
Kipper – baked	11.4	0
Mackerel – raw	16.3	0
Pilchards – canned in tomato sauce	5.4	0
Salmon – raw	(12.0)	0
steamed	13.0	0
canned	8.2	0
smoked	4.5	0
Sardines – fresh, raw	8.6	0
canned in oil, fish only	13.6	0
canned in tomato sauce	11.6	0
Trout – rainbow, steamed	3.8	0
Tuna – fresh, raw	4.4	0
canned in oil	22.0	0
canned in brine	0.6	0
Whitebait – fried	47.5	0

	Fat g	Fibre g
Other Seafood		
Crab – boiled	5.2	0
canned	0.9	0
Lobster – boiled	3.4	0
Prawns – boiled	1.8	0
Scampi – fried	17.6	0
Shrimps – boiled	2.4	0
Cockles – boiled	0.3	0
Mussels – boiled	2.0	0
Oysters – raw	0.9	0
Scallops – steamed	1.4	0
Whelks – boiled	1.9	0
Winkles – boiled	1.4	0
Squid – raw	0.8	0
Swordfish – raw	4.0	0

	Fat g	Fibre g
Fish products		
Fish cakes – fried	10.5	0
Fish fingers – fried	12.7	0
Fish paste	10.4	0

MEAT AND MEAT PRODUCTS

	Fat g	Fibre g
Bacon – lean, raw	7.4	0
fat, raw	80.9	0
rashers, grilled, lean only	18.9	0
middle, lean and fat	35.1	0
Beef – lean, raw	4.6	0
mince, raw	16.2	0
rump steak, fried, lean and fat	14.6	0
lean only	7.4	0
grilled, lean and fat	12.1	0
lean only	6.0	0
sirloin, roast, lean only	9.1	0
topside, roast, lean only	4.4	0
Lamb – chops, grilled, lean and fat	29.0	0
lean only	12.3	0
cutlets, grilled, lean and fat	30.9	0
lean only	12.3	0
leg, roast, lean and fat	17.9	0
lean only	8.1	0
Pork – lean, raw	7.1	0
fat, raw	71.4	0
chops, grilled, lean and fat	24.2	0
lean only	10.7	0
leg, roast, lean and fat	19.8	0
lean only	6.9	0

	Fat g	Fibre g
Poultry and game		
Chicken – raw, meat only	4.3	0
meat and skin	17.7	0
roast, meat only	5.4	0
meat and skin	14.0	0
Duck – roast, meat only	9.7	0
meat, fat and skin	29.0	0
Goose – roast	22.4	0
Grouse – roast	5.3	0
Partridge – roast	7.2	0
Pheasant – roast	9.3	0
Turkey – raw, meat only	2.2	0
meat and skin	6.9	0
roast, meat only	2.7	0
meat and skin	6.5	0
Venison – roast	6.4	0
Offal		
Kidney – lamb, raw	2.7	0
Liver – chicken, raw	6.3	0
Meat products		
Corned beef	12.1	0
Chopped ham and pork	23.6	0
Liver sausage	26.9	0
Sausages – frankfurters	25.0	0
salami	45.2	0
beef, grilled	17.3	0
pork, grilled	24.6	0
Beefburgers – frozen, raw	20.5	0
Cornish pasty	20.4	0
Pork pie – individual	27.0	0
Sausage roll – flaky pastry	36.2	0

	Fat g	Fibre g
CEREALS AND CEREAL PRODUCTS		
Bran (wheat)	5.5	44.0
Cornflour	0.7	–
Flour – wholemeal (100%)	2.0	9.6
white, plain	1.2	3.4
self-raising	1.2	3.7
Oatmeal – raw	8.7	7.0
Porridge	0.9	0.8
Rice – polished, boiled	0.3	0.8
Basmati, raw	0.5	–
brown, boiled	1.1	1.5
Spaghetti – boiled	0.3	–
wholemeal, boiled	0.9	4.0
Couscous	1.0	–
Bread – wholemeal	2.7	8.5
brown	2.2	5.1
white	1.7	2.7
Rolls – brown, crusty	3.2	(5.9)
soft	6.4	(5.4)
white, crusty	3.2	(3.1)
soft	7.3	(2.9)
Croissant	20.3	2.5
Pitta bread	1.2	3.9
Breakfast cereals – All-Bran	5.7	26.7
cornflakes	1.6	11.0
muesli	7.5	7.4
weetabix	3.4	12.7
Biscuits – chocolate full-coated	27.6	3.1
cream crackers	16.3	(3.0)
digestive plain	20.5	(5.5)
chocolate	24.1	3.5
Water biscuits	12.5	(3.2)
Cakes – fruit cake, rich	11.0	3.5
sponge cake, with fat	26.5	1.0
without fat	6.7	1.0
jam-filled	4.9	1.2

	Fat g	Fibre g
Currant buns	7.5	1.8
Doughnuts	15.8	–
Eclairs	24.0	–
Mince Pies	20.7	2.9
Pastry – choux, cooked	20.1	1.3
flaky, cooked	40.5	2.0
shortcrust, cooked	32.2	2.4
Scones	14.6	2.1
Puddings – apple crumble	6.9	2.5
bread and butter	7.8	0.6
Cheesecake	34.9	0.9
Creme Caramel	2.2	–
Ice-cream, dairy	6.6	–
non-dairy	8.2	–
Lemon Meringue pie	14.6	0.7
Lemon Sorbet	Tr	0
Meringues	0	0
Milk pudding	4.2	–
Pancakes	16.3	0.9
Yorkshire pudding	10.1	1.0

MILK AND MILK PRODUCTS / EGGS

Milk – cows, fresh, whole	3.8	0
long life (UHT treated)	3.8	0
fresh, skimmed	0.1	0
condensed, whole, sweetened	9.0	0
condensed, skimmed, sweetened	0.3	0
evaporated, whole, unsweetened	9.0	0
Butter – salted	82.0	0
Cream – single	21.2	0
double	48.2	0
whipping	35.0	0
Cheese – Brie	26.9	0

	Fat g	Fibre g
Camembert	23.2	0
Cheddar	33.5	0
Cheddar, reduced fat	15.0	0
Danish Blue	29.2	0
Edam	22.9	0
Feta	20.2	0
Gorgonzola	28.4	0
Gruyere	33.3	0
Parmesan	29.7	0
Roquefort	32.9	0
Stilton	40.0	0
cottage cheese	4.0	0
cream cheese	47.4	0
processed cheese	25.0	0
cheese spread	22.9	0
Fromage Frais – plain	7.1	0
fruit	5.8	0
very low fat	0.2	0
Yogurt – natural	1.0	0
fruit	1.0	0
Greek, cows	9.1	0
sheep	7.5	0
Eggs – whole, raw	10.9	0
white, raw	Tr	0
yolk, raw	30.5	0
boiled	10.9	0
fried	19.5	0
poached	11.7	0
omelette	16.4	0
scrambled	22.7	0

NUTS

Almonds	53.5	14.3
Barcelona nuts	64.0	10.3

	Fat g	Fibre g
Brazil nuts	61.5	9.0
Chestnuts	2.7	6.8
Cob or hazel nuts	36.0	6.1
Coconut – fresh	36.0	13.6
desiccated	62.0	23.5
Peanuts – fresh	49.0	8.1
roasted and salted	49.0	8.1
Peanut butter – smooth	53.7	7.6
Pistachio nuts	54.0	–
Walnuts	51.5	5.2

FATS AND OILS

	Fat g	Fibre g
Butter – salted	82.0	0
Lard	99.0	0
Low fat spread	40.7	0
Margarine – all kinds	81.0	0
Vegetable oils – coconut	99.9	0
corn	99.9	0
groundnut	99.9	0
olive	99.9	0
sesame seed	99.9	0
soybean	99.9	0
sunflower	99.9	0

SUGARS, PRESERVES AND CONFECTIONERY

	Fat g	Fibre g
Sugar – demerara	0	0
white	0	0
Syrup – golden	0	0
Honey – comb	4.6	–
in jars	Tr	–
Jam – fruit with edible seeds	0	1.1
Lemon curd	5.1	0.2
Marmalade	0	0.7
Marzipan – almond paste	24.9	6.4
Mincemeat	4.3	3.3
Boiled sweets	Tr	0

	Fat g	Fibre g
Chocolate – milk	30.3	–
plain	29.2	–
fancy and filled	18.8	–
Bounty Bar	26.1	–
Mars Bar	18.9	–
Fruit gums	0	–
Liquorice allsorts	2.2	–
Pastilles	0	–
Peppermints	0.7	0
Toffees – mixed	17.2	–

SAUCES, SOUPS AND MISCELLANEOUS FOODS

Sauces

	Fat g	Fibre g
Barbecue sauce	1.8	–
Bread sauce	5.0	0.5
Brown sauce – bottled	Tr	–
Cheese sauce	14.6	0.2
Chilli sauce	0.6	–
Chutney – apple	0.1	1.8
French dressing	73.0	0
Mayonnaise – ordinary	78.9	0
reduced calorie	28.1	–
Salad cream – ordinary	27.4	–
reduced calorie	17.2	–
Soy sauce – dark, thick	0.6	–
light, thin	0.5	–
Tomato ketchup	Tr	–
Tomato puree	Tr	–

Soups

	Fat g	Fibre g
Chicken – cream of, canned	3.8	–
Lentil	3.7	2.2
Minestrone – dried, as served	0.7	0.5
Mushroom – cream of, canned	3.8	–

	Fat g	Fibre g
Tomato – cream of, canned	3.3	–
Vegetable – canned	0.7	–

Miscellaneous

	Fat g	Fibre g
Baking powder	Tr	–
Bovril	0.7	0
Curry powder	10.8	–
Gelatin	Tr	0
Marmite	0.7	–
Mustard powder	28.7	–
Pepper	6.5	–
Salt – table	0.0	0
Vinegar	0.0	0
Yeast – dried	1.5	(21.9)

CHAPTER 6

THE WALKER'S WORK-OUT

The wise for cure on exercise depend
JOHN DRYDEN

A warm-up routine is vital before brisk aerobic walking, because sudden vigorous activity can cause the heart to act abnormally. It can also lead to sprains, and torn muscles, tendons and ligaments.

Muscles work much better when relaxed, and it is much easier to find your stride and get into a good walking rhythm. The warm-up stretches that follow in the quick routine, take only a few minutes, and should always be done before brisk walking. They relax the huge muscle on the front of the thigh (the quadriceps), the hamstring muscles at the back of the thigh, and the back of the calves and the Achilles tendons. They are followed by a further four warm-up stretches which you can do if you have the time. After these warm-up stretches, there are 20 stretches that provide you with flexibility and strength.

Walking is an excellent way of exercising the main muscle mass of the body (two-thirds of which is in the legs), and it will give you a good aerobic cardiovascular work-out. But to achieve total body fitness you need to exercise all the main muscle groups in the body. The stretches for flexibility and strength will help you do this. A good workout several times a week will complement your aerobic walking routine and will help you build long term fitness.

The body is naturally designed to be flexible and to move and stretch easily. However, if you have been sedentary for some time and are not used to bending and stretching movements, then you are likely to be stiff and out of condition. You should approach the exercises for flexibility and strength with caution. You cannot expect to achieve all these positions as you start out, any more than you can expect to walk aerobically for 45 minutes when you first begin.

Let the movements flow naturally; perform them slowly and smoothly and don't overstretch. Ease into them gently. As you perform each exercise, slowly stretch into the position, going only as far as is comfortable. If it begins to hurt then ease back or stop. If you find the number of repetitions too many to begin with, then reduce them to what you find comfortable.

Like your aerobic walking, these exercises should leave you feeling relaxed and revitalised, not tired and aching. If you feel tired and aching afterwards, then you are overdoing them. The key to performing them is to stretch slowly into them, letting the movements flow naturally.

If you have a specific back, neck or other problem that may prevent you from performing any of the stretching exercises in this chapter, then you should consult your family doctor before trying them – show him the exercises and ask his advice.

Cooling-down exercises after aerobic walking are just as important as warming-up exercises. Gradually reduce your pace as you come to the end of your walk. This will help you to avoid post-exercise stiffness and you will suffer from far less sore muscles. Then do the cool-down exercises, finishing with the total relaxation exercise.

Quadriceps Stretch – grasp right foot with both hands behind you, and pull, feeling tension along front of thigh. Hold for 10–20 seconds then switch legs.

Lying Hamstring Stretch – bend right knee, placing foot flat on floor. Bend left knee and hold gently under knee. Pull left leg gently towards chest. Hold for 10–20 seconds then switch legs.

Achilles and Calf Stretch – start facing a wall, hands pressed against it. Bend one knee forward holding opposite leg straight. Hold for 10–20 seconds then switch legs.

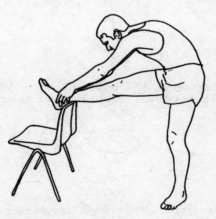

Standing Hamstring Stretch – place leg over top of chair, parallel to the ground and stretch arms to touch toes. Hold for 10–20 seconds then switch legs.

Raise arms overhead. Allow head to roll back freely, then stretch backwards, with hips pushed forward. Repeat 5 times.

Lie with back flat on floor pelvis tucked in, legs together outstretched. Breathing deeply from abdomen, pull knees towards head. Repeat 5 times.

Side Bends – with feet apart, lean to one side, other, sliding your hand down leg. Repeat 5 times then switch legs.

Arm Circling – circle both arms, reaching up above head, then out and down to complete circle. Breathe in as arms lift, out as they come down. Repeat 5 times.

STRETCHES FOR FLEXIBILITY
AND STRENGTH

Lie flat on floor, knees bent, arms by your side. Pull your stomach in and breathe deeply from abdomen for 10 seconds.

Then lift buttocks off floor by contracting them and using your stomach muscles. Hold for 5 seconds. Repeat 5 times.

Lie on your back, feet pointing to ceiling, knees slightly bent,
arms by your sides. Using abdominal muscles, raise head
and upper torso, exhaling as you reach forward with hands
past your thighs. Inhale and relax back without letting head
touch floor. Repeat 5 times.

Kneel, sitting on your heels. Lean backwards putting hands
flat on floor behind your feet. Relax neck, letting head fall
backwards. Tighten bottom and push abdomen upward,
raising bottom off heels. Repeat 5 times.

Lie on your back, feet together, palms flat on floor. Raise legs and make splits movements 5 times. Lower legs until they almost touch floor and repeat exercise 5 times, relaxing between.

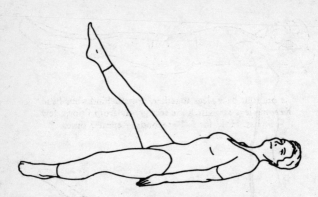

Lie on your back, arms outstretched. Slowly raise then lower each leg alternately, counting 5 to raise, 5 to hold and 5 to lower. Repeat 5 times, relaxing between.

Cycling – lie on floor, raising legs in the air, supporting hips with hands. Do cycling movement while counting to 10.

Lie on your back, legs together, arms behind your head.
Keeping legs straight, raise feet gently from floor a few
inches. Hold for 5–10 seconds. Repeat 5 times.

From legs together position, slowly raise top leg as far as
you can. Hold for count of 5 then slowly lower. Repeat 5
times.

Keeping legs together, slowly raise them. Hold for count of
5 then slowly lower. Repeat 5 times. Turn over and repeat
both movements, 5 times each.

Lie face down, elbows bent, hands on floor. Straighten arms, pushing forward on hands so that head and chest are pushed upward without straining. Hold for 10 seconds, then relax. Repeat 5 times.

Lie on floor, hands by side. Raise left leg slowly, then lower. Repeat 5 times then switch legs.

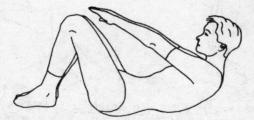

Sit, legs outstretched. Place right foot over left leg, then place right hand behind you and hold left knee with left hand. Slowly twist to right. Stretch body and turn head as far as possible. Do 3 twists then change over legs; left foot over right leg and repeat exercise.

Lie on your back with knees bent. Gently pull your upper body up as far as possible, arms outstretched reaching towards knees. Hold for count of 5. Repeat 5 times.

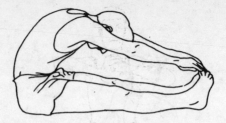

Sit with back straight, legs together, breathing deeply. Slowly
lean forward to touch your toes, breathing out, relaxing at
same time. Repeat 5 times.

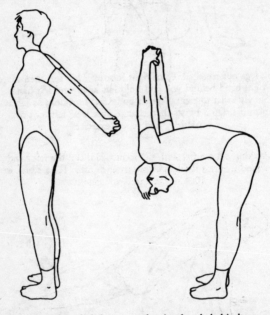

Stand with feet slightly apart, clasping hands behind you,
keeping arms straight. Slowly lift them up without bending
forwards. Feel the pull of the chest muscles.

Now bend forwards keeping hands clasped. Let head hang
and raise arms as high as possible. Straighten up and repeat
5 times.

Making a loose fist with the right hand, cup the left hand around it. Press the hands against each other for a count of 10. Change hands and repeat.

Push-ups – lie face down, palms flat beside shoulders and toes tucked under. Breathe in, then, breathing out, push up as far as possible. Breathe in and lower to floor. Repeat 5–10 times.

WARM-DOWN STRETCHES

Lean forward from waist, breathing out. Let arms hang
loosely. Straighten up and repeat 5 times.

Side bends – with feet apart, lean to one side, other, sliding
your hand down leg. Repeat 5 times then switch legs.

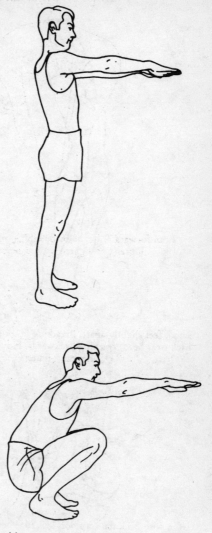

From standing position, arms outstretched, squat, keeping
arms parallel to ground. Repeat 10 times.

Stand, feet slightly apart. Breathing in, bring hands up and
back over head, reaching backwards. Hold for count of 5.
Repeat 5 times.

Lie with back flat on floor, legs together outstretched.
Breathing deeply from abdomen, pull knees towards head.
Repeat 5 times.

Shoulder Stand – lie on your back, feet together, legs straight.
Brace hands against hips and raise trunk and legs above
head. Relax and breathe normally. Hold for 1–2 minutes.

Total Relaxation – lie flat on back, knees bent, arms at sides
and support the back of head with books piled to height of
about 4 inches. Breathe deeply from abdomen and
concentrate on relaxing every part of the body. Start with
the toes and say to yourself 'my toes are completely and
totally relaxing'. Work up through the rest of the body: the
legs, stomach, chest, back, shoulders, to the head, using the
same relaxing words, but using your own version. A total
relaxation session can last from 5 to 15 minutes or longer.

CHAPTER 7

WALK AWAY FROM STRESS

Walk and be happy,
Walk and be healthy.
CHARLES DICKENS

Two of the main problems of living in modern Western society are:

1. Being tense, anxious and stressful.
2. Sitting around much of the day (being sedentary).

This leads some people to the view that modern life itself is a disease, which expresses itself in obsessive work, anger, cynicism, fatigue, an inner hunger that nothing can fill, overeating, excessive smoking and alcoholism – often symptoms of dis-ease with oneself and the world.

Tension is something that we all feel from time to time – our muscles are wound up, our brain is overworked, we feel fatigued and overwrought. Tension is a symptom of anxiety, the 'fight or flight' response of primitive survival behaviour.

In primitive times danger often meant anxiety, and anxiety provided the energy to respond effectively with 'fight or flight'. That was fine for primitive man, but the choice for modern man in industrialised Western civilisation is not as simple. How can he choose between 'fight or flight' if he feels cornered, ill-equipped and uncertain about which course of action to take.

We live in an age of uncertainty: an age of rapid change with increasing pressures and the need to survive. Some people call it the psycho-toxic society where the chief protagonist in the drama is 'stress'.

Stress, we are told, is now held to be the number one killer in the Western world and in Britain alone stress-related absenteeism costs British industry £2 billion a year. Mental stress and illness cost British industry 37 million lost days each year and a MORI survey suggests that worry and stress account for 77 per cent of all mental disorders. And in the USA, estimates for the combined cost to industry of absenteeism, low productivity, health charges and increased insurance are said to be $75 billion.

These days, not only is work, divorce, retirement and bereavement stressful, but getting married we are told is also stressful. Taking holidays is stressful – even dieting, exercise and the quest for fitness are stressful.

We talk about 'stress management'. We attend stress relief classes, meditation centres, positive thinking classes. Some people take up juggling; others spend time in flotation tanks trying to relax.

The basis of most stress is anxiety and emotional conflict. Stressful conditions sooner or later translate into bodily symptoms causing tension, aching joints, headaches and backache, insomnia and depression.

Stress destroys essential vitamins and minerals and lowers the body's immune response. It triggers fatigue and leads to biochemical changes in our bodies. Unchecked, these biochemical changes can damage our heart and vascular system resulting in high blood pressure, strokes and other diseases.

CAN WE AVOID STRESS?

How do we break away from stress, from 'the thousand natural shocks that flesh is heir to' as Shakespeare put it?

We don't. We can no more avoid stress than we can avoid eating, drinking or breathing. Stress is part of life. And stress (good stress) can be motivating and stimulating. It is only a problem when it gets on top of us: when it is out of control (bad stress).

Bad stress is often associated with anxiety, fear, overwork, insomnia, boredom, grief and poor self-image. Taken to extremes it can lead to debilitating illness. Good stress, on the other hand, is encountered when we meet challenging situations (meeting new people, a job interview, making a public speech) or when we push ourselves to get things done.

Modern living is by its very nature fragmentary and specialised. The problem began with the Scientific Revolution in the 16th and 17th centuries. In order to understand the structure of Nature, man began to dissect everything that came under his control.

And then the problem developed further with the Industrial Revolution in the late 18th and early 19th centuries, when people left the land in increasing numbers to work in the towns. Division of labour often took away the satisfaction and personal worth felt by the individual craftsman and made him feel that he was no more than a cog in a machine.

Although these revolutions have helped put

men on the moon and given us the life-saving advances of modern medicine, on their negative side they have often left modern man in a state of alienation with himself, his neighbour and the society he lives in. Stress is only one expression of the loss of balance felt by modern man.

The philosopher Plato suggests in his famous allegory that we are all like prisoners in a cave, and that what we take to be real are only shadows thrown upon the wall of the cave by a fire.

We spend too much time inside our heads; too much time inside buildings; too much time inside houses and cars. Remember the folk song that Pete Seeger used to sing:

Little boxes, little boxes,
Little boxes made of ticky tacky,
Little boxes, little boxes,
Little boxes all the same.

We need to get out: get outside of our heads, get outside of the artificial cocoons we have surrounded ourselves with, get out into the open air where the perspective is clear and we can see into the distance, beyond the windows and the four walls around us, and the people inside them.

Instead of trying to break away from stress what we should be doing is trying to neutralise its harmful effects. Like a tightrope walker, each day we tread the perilous road between good stress and bad stress. For some people it is not a problem; but for increasing numbers of people it is a problem – a dead end street with no way out. They lose their balance on the tightrope and fall off.

SEDENTARY MAN UNDER STRESS

Not only do we now have the psycho-toxic society, but we have the hypo-kinetic society and hypo-kinetic disease: disease resulting from too little physical activity.

Dr Hans Selye is the scientist who put the word 'stress' into our scientific language. In his well-known experiment, he took ten sedentary laboratory rats and subjected them to blinding lights, electric shocks and incessant noise. In a month they were all dead. He took a further ten rats and exercised them regularly on a treadmill, then subjected them to the same stressful conditions. A month later they were all alive and thriving. Exercise had given them the psychological edge to cope with stress.

In human beings there is a paradox of exercise: as more exercise is taken, then more energy becomes available. The body seems to like being stretched; it moves into 'overdrive', and it is this regular stretching that allows both human beings and animals to cope with stress.

However, as so many human beings in Western society are sedentary, it is hardly any wonder that their bodies are increasingly at the mercy of stressful conditions, cardiovascular and respiratory disease and orthopaedic problems. We would not treat a dog the way we treat ourselves. Imagine what Fido would be like if you only took him out for a walk once a week.

We have to break out of the routines and habits that hold us in their power and sap our vital energy. This is what the true meaning of exercise really is. It comes from the Latin word 'ex-acere' meaning to break out from a shut-in state.

Some people try to relieve stress by playing

games such as squash, golf, tennis or bowling; or
they swim or take a holiday to get away from it
all. All these activities no doubt lift the spirits, but
the trouble with them all is that they are intermit-
tent, anaerobic, start-stop activities. None of these
activities has the stress-relieving quality of brisk,
continuous, rhythmic walking.

Walking is a holistic experience. Walking dis-
perses the ingrained patterns of physical inactivity
and stress. Walking is a totally natural expression
of the human body both physically and mentally.

WALKING – THE PERFECT EXERCISE

Walking normally we see the world at up to 3 miles
an hour. But when we put our feet down for a
brisk aerobic walk we increase our speed up to
3.5–4.0 miles an hour.

Our bodies are designed for action and movement not for sitting, standing, sauntering and strolling. As we walk, the spine flexes with each stride
then springs back again. Our feet work like the
suspension on a motor car, the arched support of
each foot absorbing the impact of weight as it
makes contact with the road surface. Then as we
begin to move, the forward pull of the torso
becomes the engine to propel us forward under the
force of gravity. With each stride first one, then
the other leg swings out on its ball-and-socket hip
joint as the muscles in the feet, legs, hips, back,
shoulder and neck all work rhythmically together
like the players in a symphony orchestra.

All of this is perfectly natural like the flight
of a bird or the movement of a fish through water.
Walking does not strain and pull the muscles and
ligaments as jogging can; it does not overstretch
and overdevelop the legs as cycling can. The body

moves rhythmically through space in the way it was designed to do three million years ago.

Professor Owen Lovejoy, an anthropologist at Kent State University in the USA, has made the following observation, quoted in *Scientific American*, on walking and its place in man's development:

'Asked to choose the most distinctive feature of the human species, many people would cite our massive brain. Others might mention our ability to make and use sophisticated tools. A third feature also sets us apart: our upright mode of locomotion, which is found only in human beings and our immediate ancestors ... The development of erect walking may have been a crucial initiating event in human evolution.'

We used to believe that man had been walking upright for between one and two million years. Professor Lovejoy went on to suggest that upright walking could date back 3 million years and possibly some 8 or 10 million years, to the earliest hominids. Why then, after evolution has worked so hard to perfect the human body, is homo sapiens going out of its way to turn back the clock and undo all those years of fine tuning done by evolution?

A PSYCHO-PHYSICAL TONIC

It is brisk, aerobic walking that can break down the cycle of stress and tension that is the bugbear of life in the late 20th century. By the rhythmic action of the muscles, stress and tension are drained off and dissipated, and the body is restored to its natural state of equilibrium. It is this sense of rhythm that is described here by Tom Chetwynd in his book, *A Dictionary of Symbols*:

'Inner turmoil, conflict, confusion leads directly to walking . . . walking restores a sense of balance and brings an inner calm . . . is archetypally symbolic . . . the left foot alternates with the right, the conscious side with the unconscious side, between heart (the emotional life, the feminine side) on the left of the body and reason on the right, and so between the opposing pressures which caused the turmoil in the first place. The action of walking erect and balanced, like a vertical line, the world axis, can unite conscious and unconscious, mind and matter, in a way that thinking never can.'

Walking is the perfect way to relax. You can use it to disperse tension or to prevent tension. Outside on the road, the mind and body find their own rhythm, not the rhythm imposed on them by circumstances. They are no longer playing second string to other discordant rhythms; they are on their own. Outside on the road it is a solo performance.

As you feel the rhythm and movement in your feet, calves, thighs, arms and shoulders, you will begin to let go, to truly let go and flow with it all. Your breathing will deepen naturally and become more regular and your circulation will respond as fresh oxygenated blood flows around your body.

Negative emotions will drain away while you walk. Problems that have been nagging away at your mind will be solved in an instant. The Greek philosopher Socrates used to talk about: '. . . the blessed fruit of the vine which reduces great disasters into small inconveniences.' We can say the same about walking. Walking takes hold of the linear patterns of much of our daily thinking, and reorders them in a holistic way. Seemingly insoluble problems melt away during the continuous rhythmic flow of walking. Tension and stress become things of the past.

RHYTHMIC BREATHING

Walking is as natural as breathing and breathing is as natural as walking. To breathe is to live and without breath there is no life. Life is a series of breaths: from the first breath of the infant to the last gasp of the dying man.

We can exist for a time without eating; we can exist for a shorter time without drinking; but without breathing our life will be cut short after a few minutes. What really matters to us is the quality of our breathing, and it is here that we can make a significant contribution in assisting our mind and body to free themselves from tension and anxiety.

Although breathing deepens naturally as we walk, we may still be taking in less oxygen if we are breathing mainly from the chest area rather than using deep rhythmic breathing from the diaphragm. This is the type of breathing used in the practice of meditation and Yoga.

Efficient breathing through the nostrils pulls the air deep into the lungs, expanding the lungs downward, and the lungs and chest outward. To breathe deeply, inhale by first moving your abdomen outwards. You will feel your stomach rise, then your upper abdomen, and finally your chest. Then breathe out by letting your stomach relax. It may feel strange at first, but this is the way that most of us breathe when we sleep.

Slow deep rhythmic breathing can double the volume of air you inhale with each breath, and together with brisk aerobic walking, it is the first step to attaining full relaxation and increased awareness. Deep rhythmic breathing will revitalise you. Muscles will relax and the mind will clear, as tension and stress are drained away and you let go totally.

As you increase your walking pace, you may want to try linking your breathing to it. For example: breathe in, counting (mentally) 1, 2, 3, 4, 5, 6, 7, 8, one count to each step, making the inhalation extend over the eight counts. Then exhale slowly through the nostrils, counting as before – 1, 2, 3, 4, 5, 6, 7, 8 – one count to each step. Rest between breaths and then continue at will. Experiment: you may find that counting to 4 or 6 or even 10 may suit you better. Counting breaths helps you to focus on a single idea, and it is an effective stress releaser. It is covered further in the next chapter under 'Walking Meditation'.

You may want to try what we call energy breathing. This really gets you going when you feel sluggish. Do the same exercise above, but instead of exhaling through the nostrils, exhale through the mouth: breathe in through the nostrils counting 1 to 8, then out through the mouth counting 1 to 8.

Another tension releaser is to get into a rhythmic stride and concentrate on relaxing each part of the body in turn. Start out by saying to yourself 'my toes are relaxing . . . my feet are relaxing . . . my legs are relaxing . . .' and so on up through your body until you reach the top of your head. Say to yourself 'the tensions and troubles of the day are all draining out of my body . . . I feel totally at peace with myself and the world . . . I feel terrific.'

Don't laugh! It really does work. It's called 'autogenics', which means instructions made to yourself by yourself. It became popular with Emile Coue's 'every day in every way I am getting better, and better, and better.' It is now very popular as a way of reaching deep relaxation, and there are even Autogenic Centres where you can learn more about it. Try it, but don't use my words – use your own.

THE ANSWER TO STRESS

By now you should be walking regularly for health, fitness and slimness; and you will have noticed the effect that walking has on helping you to relax, whatever time of the day it is.

The body has its own rhythms, regulating temperature, hunger, mood, and alertness. It is these rhythms which explain why most people are sluggish early in the morning, and why they are much more alert later in the day. Body rhythms can be affected by many factors: food, drink, drugs, smoking, and lack of sleep. But the good news is that we can control our body rhythms (our body clocks) by brisk aerobic walking.

MORNING WALKS – Walk aerobically first thing in the morning for between 15 and 30 minutes to prepare yourself for the day ahead. Even if you only have time for a ten minute walk, you will experience immediately the relaxing effect of getting out of the house away from telephones, people, and the throb of civilisation. You will feel your body 'getting into gear' for the day as it takes in fresh supplies of oxygen and begins working like the efficient machine it is meant to be.

Walking first thing in the morning boosts your body temperature, makes you feel more alert and breaks those 'early morning blues'. But you must warm up thoroughly before walking, especially in the morning, and take it a little easier than usual –

strolling for a few minutes before getting into a brisk stride.

Walk to work if you can, or get off your bus or train a few stops earlier and walk the rest of the way. Walk to your local shops rather than take a vehicle.

AFTERNOON WALKS – Tension and anxiety often build up through the day, so lunchtime and afternoon walks can drain them off leaving you feeling refreshed for the rest of the working day.

Instead of sitting around at lunchtime, go for a brisk aerobic walk for at least 20 minutes, then eat a light Walking Diet lunch. There is a lot of evidence to suggest that exercise depresses the appetite and helps with weight control.

Late afternoon can be peak anxiety time and can leave you feeling fatigued and listless at the end of the working day. If you live near work then walk home. If you are catching a bus or train then walk a few stops before getting on. Alternatively, get off a few stops earlier and walk the rest of the way.

EVENING WALKS – The evening may be the time that you choose to do your main aerobic walking; in which case it is better to walk before your evening meal to gain the maximum benefit from it. But if you have already knocked up the necessary aerobic miles for the day, you may want to use an evening walk to reflect on the day and use a quiet walk as a way of de-stressing.

Walking has a tranquillising effect on the mind and it drains off the muscular tension in the body that has built up during the working day. After an evening walk you will be ready to retire to bed for a sound, uninterrupted night's sleep. There is

evidence to suggest that walking in the evening
may help insomnia.

WALKING BREAKS – Next time you stop for a
tea or coffee break, or stop to have a cigarette,
change your mind and go for a ten minute walk
instead. Not only will your body thank you for it
– caffeine is a stimulant and increases tension, and
nicotine is a poison – but you will actually feel
better for it.

MUSIC WHILE YOU WALK – Some people like
to take a Walkman with them on their aerobic
walks. They find that the rhythm of certain types
of music helps them to walk at a steady pace and
achieve a state of deep relaxation. Classical music,
marches, swing, country, and pop music can all
help dissolve stress.

The mind is a human instrument and physical
and mental health can be affected by certain types
of music. The composer Mendelssohn said: 'Music
cannot be expressed in words, not because it is
vague but because it is more precise than words.'
Used with an aerobic walking schedule, music can
help unlock the cycle of stress and produce a state
of calm.

Experiments have shown that Baroque music
(composed in the second half of the 17th and first
half of the 18th centuries) can particularly have a
deep calming and relaxing effect on the mind.

Just remember, that if you listen to music
while you walk, then look where you are going. It
may not be such a good idea to do it if you are
walking in a busy urban area.

WALKING WITH OTHERS – Walking with a
friend can help motivate you to build up a regular

aerobic routine and can also help you to de-stress after a hard day's work. The continuous rhythmic effect of walking dissolves stress and clears the mind. It is only when the mind and body are fully relaxed in this way that problems are simplified and solutions present themselves.

It is often said that a problem shared is a problem halved. Talk through the problems of the day and look for creative solutions to them. People who have good friends to talk to, don't usually need psychiatrists.

One research organisation has suggested that the reason that many people give up exercising is because of marriage and family commitments. People with this problem should try walking. Walking is the easiest exercise of all to share with others. Walk with your spouse, your children, and your relatives. How many problems in the home, we wonder, could be solved simply by taking a walk. If you find yourself in conflict with your spouse, children or in-laws, then take them for a walk. Out there on the road, troubles dissolve, and you can find the time and space to put them into perspective.

Walk in the morning before tension becomes a problem, and walk at lunchtime to dispel the tensions of the morning. Walk in the early evening before dinner and walk before retiring to bed. The Dutch theologian Erasmus used to say: 'Before supper walk a little; after supper do the same.' Walk on your own or walk with others. Whatever the time of day, walk for the sheer joy and relax-ation of walking. Whichever way you look at it, the best stress therapy is walking.

CHAPTER 8

THE ART OF WALKING

Afoot and light-hearted I take to the open road,
Healthy, free, the world before me,
The long brown path before me leading wherever I choose.

Henceforth I ask not good fortune, I myself am good fortune,
Henceforth I whimper no more, postpone no more, need nothing,
Done with indoor complaints, libraries, querulous criticisms,
Strong and content I travel the open road.

'LEAVES OF GRASS' – WALT WHITMAN

There is a need for us all to renew ourselves from time to time and take stock of who we are and where we are going. There are many ways to do this. Some people turn to organised religion and prayer, others to Eastern methods such as Yoga and Zen Buddhism. Yet others seek enlightenment in depth psychology and Art.

Earlier in this book we introduced the Greek idea of 'diata', and suggested that health and fitness is about much more than extreme diet and exercise routines; it is in fact a whole way of life. We have looked in detail about how to achieve the fit, healthy bodies and minds that we all desire. But life is surely about more than simply having a healthy mind in a healthy body.

'Know thyself,' the Greek philosopher Socrates said. 'If I am not myself, who else will be?' the walking philosopher and writer Thoreau said.

The longest journey we ever make is the journey within. We may use one of the more traditional methods to come to a greater realisation of ourselves and discover a deeper meaning of life, or we may improvise our own methods using one or all of the above disciplines. The important thing is the realisation that we need to make the journey if we are to be whole.

Some people use prayer, others use meditation and yoga techniques to prepare for the journey inward. The one thing that they all have in common is the need for total relaxation: a letting go of obsessive thoughts and all the clutter and confusion going on in the mind.

So where do we start?

'The way out is via the door.' (Lao-Tse)

WALKING MEDITATION

Once you have discovered the benefits of aerobic walking for health, fitness and slimness, you will want to go further and discover the additional benefits provided by inner walking.

Inner walking is walking meditation, and it begins with relaxation and the feeling of letting go. Inner walking has nothing to do with goals or objectives. Use aerobic walking to get fit, improve your CV system and lose weight; use inner walking to encounter a deeper self-knowledge, greater concentration and serenity.

You can use walking meditation to break the pattern of obsessive thoughts and tension. You can use it to centre yourself inside your own experience and give yourself an overview of what is happening inside – what is really happening, not what you thought was happening. Walking meditation will give you control over your life.

How does it work?

There is a saying that the mind is like a drunken monkey. Think for a moment about the daily traffic of sounds going on inside your head, from the minute that you wake up to the minute that you go to bed. Think about the constant voice-over in your mind as a continuous sound track superimposed on an endlessly rolling film.

That is what the mind is like much of the time. And then think what it would be like to slow it all down and feel that it is you that is in control, and not the machinery that is controlling you.

The key to walking meditation is to keep your mind focused on what you are doing. You may be able to do this by simply walking for a while and letting the feeling of deep relaxation take over and provide the focus that you seek. Or you may want to use one of the traditional meditation methods to help you. You could try counting steps or counting breaths, or you could try using a mantra.

Counting your footsteps is a simple method to keep you in the here and now. You can count up to 10, 20, or a 100, either forwards or backwards, repeating it over and over. If that becomes a habit then try the following method:

1. Count your first seven steps.

2. With your next step, begin at 1 and count to 8.

3. Then with your next step, begin at 1 and count to 9.

4. Continue in the same way until you reach 12.

5. Repeat the sequence from the beginning as many times as you like.

Counting your breaths is another meditation which is easy to do. As you walk, count your exhalations up to 10 and begin again. If that becomes a habit, then instead of simply counting breaths you could pick out a lamp post or a tree a couple of hundred yards along the road and count your breaths until you get there. This helps to 'anchor the mind' and focus awareness.

Using a mantra is another popular meditational practice. A mantra is a word or phrase that you can repeat to focus your awareness. 'Om' is the most well known and is supposed to be 'the eternal word', the basic sound of the universe. Any word or phrase that you can repeat to yourself as you walk along will do the job, but try to pick something that means something to you. Some people use words like 'love' and 'peace' – others use phrases such as 'be still and know that I am God' or 'love one another'.

The easiest way to experience walking meditation is simply to concentrate on the body movements you make. Feel the weight of your heel as it makes contact with the ground, and the spring of your toe as the muscles in your leg propel you forward. Feel the rhythm of your arms and the movement of your head and all the sensory input that is going on. Feel the stillness in movement.

Meditation is about increased awareness, concentration and self-knowledge. Whether you relax naturally into it, or use one of the above methods, go with the flow. If you find your mind wandering, gently bring it back to the task of involving yourself more and more in it. Find a walking rhythm to suit you and stick with it.

Do the meditation as long as you need to. You are not working towards a goal. All you are trying to do is relax and centre your mind. If you can do that, then you will be able to get away from the hurly burly of life any time you want to.

Another form of walking meditation is the thinking walk: the walk to help you solve a problem. Writers, artists, philosophers and all types of creative people have used the thinking walk to help them with their work. They have spoken about the magical effect of walking and of how walking can act almost like a drug in its ability to free the mind and release its creative thought processes. The swinging, rhythmic action of walking drains off tension and anxiety and allows the mind to give total attention to the act of thinking, in a way that, for example, sitting in a chair thinking can never do. Try it. Next time you have a problem, take it with you for a walk and allow the action of the whole body and mind to sort it out for you. You will be amazed. Problems that seemed insoluble will simply melt away. And if you have personal problems you want to sort out with other people, ask them to join you for a walk. You will find that there are few problems that cannot be solved by taking a half-hour walk and talking things through.

Why should this be so? Walking, as we have already discovered, increases the supply of oxygen throughout our bodies. This is what makes walking an aerobic activity. And it is the increased supply of oxygen to the brain that stimulates our thought processes and enables us to see things more clearly and put them into perspective.

As well as the thinking walk, there is its opposite: the non-thinking walk – the Zen walk. During this walk, instead of consciously thinking through problems, the intention is to walk without thinking, to deliberately empty the conscious mind and allow the unconscious mind to take over and sort out the problem.

Try it out. Before your walk, go over in your mind the problem to be solved; then forget about it. Let the conscious mind relax, and let the problem go out of your mind. Don't set a time limit for a solution; the solution will come in its own good time. The unconscious mind will go on working in the background, and you will find that the answer to the problem will arise unexpectedly. It may be during the next walk you take, or the next day even. It does not matter when.

This type of problem-solving is creativity by 'serendipity' – making discoveries that you are not consciously searching for, that happen by chance or accident. During the writing of this book we would often use either the thinking walk or the Zen walk to solve a particular writing problem, or to get going again when we were stuck. A brisk walk has often provided the solution to the problem in hand and allowed us to get going again.

RHYTHMS OF CHANGE

The orchestral conductor, Sir Thomas Beecham, said that music frees us from the tyranny of the conscious mind. Walking can have the same effect. The rhythmical effect of walking has a musical quality about it, and it is the measured beat of the right foot alternating with the left that helps to break down the negative patterns of inactivity and stress.

Walking frees us from the tyranny of the conscious mind; it helps us to look inside ourselves, to see ourselves clearly, away from the noise and distractions of modern living. Inner walking is a natural therapy which promotes a sense of peace and rhythm that we all need in our lives.

Rhythm is all around us: it pervades the Universe and the natural world. Modern physics sees matter as 'being in a continuous dancing and vibrating motion whose rhythmic patterns are determined by the molecular, atomic and nuclear structures' (Fritjof Capra – *The Tao of Physics*). Some mystics, philosophers and poets also see the material world in the same way: as a dynamic universe that moves, vibrates and dances. When we walk we move, vibrate, and dance with it.

The composer Gustave Mahler tells the story that he was once stuck in the middle of writing a new symphony. He was stuck for weeks. No matter how hard he worked, the notes did not come. Then one day he was being rowed across a lake. Suddenly, the rhythm and movement of the oars through the water created rhythms in his own mind and the notes for the opening of the next movement came to him.

Walking can be like this. With practice, once you get into a rhythm and really begin to relax and let go, walking can stimulate a meditational state similar to the deep meditational states of Yoga and other disciplines.

I walk therefore I am. I use inner walking to be with myself: to get away from the noise and distractions of everyday life. Out there on the road the mind suddenly clears. It is lifted out of the confused chatter that often goes on inside, and it

sees as if for the first time, like a child: people,
events, trees, flowers, the stars – God.

WHO WERE THE INNER WALKERS?

Philosophers, poets, writers, musicians, and
creative people of all types have been enthusiastic
walkers – and for good reason. George Trevelyan,
who wrote the classic *History of England* said of
walking, 'I never knew a man go for an honest
day's walk for whatever distance, great or small . . .
and not have his reward in the repossession of his
soul.'

Aristotle, who was known for the Peripatetic
school of philosophy, would discourse with his
students whilst walking around the grounds of the
Academy. Emmanuel Kant walked every afternoon, and Rousseau said of his walks, 'Never have
I thought so much, never have I realized my
existence so much, I have been so much alive.'
Wordsworth, Shelley, Keats, Coleridge and de
Quincey were all inveterate walkers. It was
estimated by Wordsworth's friends that during the
course of his life he walked 185,000 miles in the
English Lake District, which inspired him to 'see
into the heart of things' and to write about:

A presence that disturbs me with the joy
Of elevated thoughts; a sense sublime
Of something far more deeply interfused,
Whose dwelling place is the light of setting
     suns,
And the round ocean, and the living air,
And the blue sky, and in the mind of man:
A motion and a spirit, that impels
All thinking things, all objects of all thought,
And rolls through all things.

.   The modern Welsh poet, R. S. Thomas, has written of a similar feeling about walking in his poem, 'The Moor':

> It was like a church to me.
> I entered it on soft foot,
> Breath held like a cap in the hand.
> It was quiet.
> What God was there made himself felt,
> Not listened to, in clean colours
> That brought a moistening of the eye,
> In movement of the wind over grass.
>
> There were no prayers said. But stillness
> Of the heart's passions – that was praise
> Enough; and the mind's cession
> Of its kingdom. I walked on,
> Simple and poor, while the air crumbled
> And broke on me generously as bread.

Dickens, Samuel Johnson, Boswell, Ruskin and Jane Austen all used their walks to free the creative mind. Beethoven and Mozart both took to the woods to discover their own 'creator spiritus'. Would Beethoven's *Pastoral Symphony* exist but for his walks in the Vienna woods? Would Mozart have given us *The Marriage of Figaro* if he had not sought inspiration in the open air? Not only men of genius, but ordinary people, have been discovering for centuries that walking has a special quality about it.

Inner walking frees us from the tyranny of the conscious mind and lets the intuitive mind breathe.

THE INTUITIVE MIND

No one really knows how intuition works, but split brain research in recent years has given us a clue. Researchers have discovered that each side of the brain, the right and the left, processes information in its own way. Although the brain as a whole works together, one side or the other tends to predominate for a specific task.

Our left brain is verbal, objective, logical, analytical, linear, and conscious, whereas our right brain is non-verbal, subjective, intuitive, holistic, spatial, and unconscious. The problem for many of us in Western society is that we tend to be left brain dominant. We live in a society which values masculine, objective, analytical skills at the expense of feminine, subjective, intuitive skills.

If we are not careful, it is easy to become trapped and blinkered in our own rational, linear thought patterns. We go on day after day in the same old way, often unhappy with our lot, but not knowing how to change it. We become stuck on a giant treadmill that turns forever without stopping.

The great Swiss psychologist, Carl Jung, summed up the modern Western way of thinking when he said that 'we think with our tongues'.

We need to give the right brain a chance. We need to free the intuitive mind. We need to let go and relax, for this has always been the first step in seeking the wholeness that we lack. You could say that we need something to inspire us. Inspire means literally 'breathe into'. We need to let go, relax, and let the intuitive mind breathe into us its spirit. We need to walk.

As you progress with inner walking and walking meditation, you will experience moments when you feel that everything suddenly becomes clear – as though you 'grasp this sorry scheme of things entire'. At such moments life is filled with a significance which it normally lacks.

Inner walkers have described the feeling as follows:

> When I am alone, as it were, completely myself . . .
> walking after a good meal . . . ideas flow best and
> most abundantly. Whence and how they come, I
> know not; nor can I force them.
>
> Wolfgang Amadeus Mozart

> I can see the whole of it at a single glance in my
> mind . . . All the inventing and making goes on in
> me in a beautiful strong dream. But the best of all
> is the hearing of it all at once.
>
> Wolfgang Amadeus Mozart

> As I went along, thinking nothing in particular,
> only looking at things around me and following
> the progress of the seasons, there would flow into
> my mind, with sudden and unaccountable emo-
> tion, sometimes a line or two of verse, sometimes
> a whole stanza at once.
>
> A. E. Houseman

JOURNEYS IN INNER TIME

There are few times when we are really alone with
ourselves. We are always too busy. We say that we
never have time. And yet we make time for almost
everything else: eating, drinking, working, making
love, entertainment and sleeping.

Time seems to be an elusive element in our
lives which tends to get out of control, and if we
are not careful it ends up controlling us. Time
measures change: change between one hour and
the next, one day and the next, and so on. In the
short run we talk about having no time, losing
time, spending time. In the long run, as the great
economist Maynard Keynes said, we are all dead.

And yet despite the fact that time can be elusive and can appear to control us, there are times, rare occasions, when we catch a glimpse of something greater, more meaningful – times when we are totally alive and whole. It can happen listening to a piece of music, reading a poem, watching a film, falling in love, staring at the stars. On such occasions we become unaware of time. We talk about time 'standing still'. Certainly time slows down, and we become unconscious of it.

We have all experienced the feeling of time distortion. Waiting for a bus or train, we are conscious that time is passing very slowly: five minutes can seem like 20. And yet when we become fully absorbed in something that interests us, we experience the opposite: an hour can seem like ten minutes.

This is because time, clock time, is a phenomenon of the conscious left brain. Waiting for a train, we are still carrying around with us all the 'mental baggage' of the day: we may be tense, angry, even fearful. Time drags. But when we do something that fully absorbs us, we let go of all the 'mental baggage' and relax. It is only then, when we fully relax and let go, that time appears to stand still and life becomes more meaningful.

Unless you are an ardent jogger, 20 minutes jogging may seem endless to you. You go out all keyed up to get fit, but the effort required is too great. You are anchored in your conscious mind. You are anxious for results. Time drags.

Walking, either brisk aerobic walking or inner walking, can produce the opposite effect. You can walk for 20 minutes and it can seem like five. You can walk for one hour and it can seem like 20 minutes. Time does not drag; you lose track of time. You are in another dimension.

To understand time we need to grasp that

there are three different kinds of time, and that we live constantly in three separate time zones.

There is social time which we can also call clock time: experienced time, time that is measured in minutes, hours, days, and weeks; time which we organise our lives by in Filofaxes and train schedules. Time for birth, growth and death.

There is cosmic time, or Nature time, which we experience as the infinite: the expanding universe, the 15 million years back to the Big Bang; the seasons and evolution.

And there is inner time. Inner time has nothing to do with clocks, calendars or social conditioning. It has nothing to do with the expanding universe or the seasons. Inner time is a time when we are alone. It is a time when we are truly with ourselves, when we can reflect and remember just who we are.

Inner time is what inner walking is all about. We leave behind the weight of clock time and social time and on the road we find ourselves, and discover the inscape of our deepest selves.

The story is told of a Zen master who was invited to give a lecture to his students. The students assembled in a great rectangular hall and sat waiting patiently for the master to arrive. Outside it was raining and the only sound inside the hall was the sound of the rain tapping against the roof.

When the master arrived, he sat down before them, and he too waited patiently, listening quietly to the sound of the rain tapping against the roof.

Suddenly the rain stopped. The master got up and asked the students to follow him outside. The students eagerly followed the master as he left the building and began to stride briskly away from them towards the hills in the distance, as though rapt in a trance. The students had to hurry, for the master had long legs and he was already starting to leave them behind.

They took a circular route across the hills, and then down through some woods near a stream, before returning to the great rectangular hall. During the journey, no one had spoken. And no one could remember how long they had walked or how far.

The students assembled again in the hall, and the master sat before them. They waited and waited, anxiously expecting the master to speak and impart his wisdom to them.

After a time the master quietly stood up; he said that the lecture was over, and left.

The sound of the rain needs no translation
Zen saying

THE ROAD AHEAD

Not I, not any one can travel that road for you,
You must travel it for yourself.
Walt Whitman

So what do we find on these inner walks, you might ask? If we knew the answer to that question we would know the answer to the meaning of existence itself. We walk to be alone: to discover something about ourselves that we did not know, or we had forgotten. We walk simply to be ourselves – whatever that means, for your inner walks will tell you something different to mine.

I can only tell you that the days when I do no inner walking I feel incomplete, as if something is missing. As much as possible, I try to keep my mind focused during the day on making sure that nothing prevents me from getting out and enjoying my inner walks.

Inner walking works not only while you walk, but it carries over to affect the whole of the rest of your life: your relationships, your work, your hopes and your dreams.

There is an ancient legend of a man who travelled the entire world in search of buried treasure. After a lifetime's search he returned tired and weary to his home village where a child pointed out to him that the treasure he had been seeking was inside himself.